CAMBRIDGE   MUSIC   HANDBOOKS

Berlioz: *Roméo et Juliette*

CAMBRIDGE MUSIC HANDBOOKS

GENERAL EDITOR Julian Rushton

Cambridge Music Handbooks provide accessible introductions to major musical works, written by the most informed commentators in the field.

With the concert-goer, performer and student in mind, the books present essential information on the historical and musical context, the composition, and the performance and reception history of each work, or group of works, as well as critical discussion of the music.

Other published titles

Bach: The Brandenburg Concertos MALCOLM BOYD
Bach: Mass in B Minor JOHN BUTT
Beethoven: *Missa solemnis* WILLIAM DRABKIN
Beethoven: Symphony No. 9 NICHOLAS COOK
Berg: Violin Concerto ANTHONY POPLE
Chopin: The Four Ballades JIM SAMSON
Handel: *Messiah* DONALD BURROWS
Haydn: *The Creation* NICHOLAS TEMPERLEY
Haydn: String Quartets, Op. 50 W. DEAN SUTCLIFFE
Janáček: *Glagolitic Mass* PAUL WINGFIELD
Mahler: Symphony No. 3 PETER FRANKLIN
Mendelssohn: *The Hebrides* and other overtures R. LARRY TODD
Mozart: The 'Jupiter' Symphony ELAINE SISMAN
Musorgsky: *Pictures at an Exhibition* MICHAEL RUSS
Schoenberg: *Pierrot lunaire* JONATHAN DUNSBY
Schubert: *Die schöne Müllerin* SUSAN YOUENS
Schumann: Fantasie, Op. 17 NICHOLAS MARSTON
Sibelius: Symphony No. 5 JAMES HEPOKOSKI
Strauss: *Also sprach Zarathustra* JOHN WILLIAMSON
Stravinsky: *Oedipus rex* STEPHEN WALSH

Berlioz: *Roméo et Juliette*

Julian Rushton

West Riding Professor of Music,
The University of Leeds

Published by the Press Syndicate of the University of Cambridge
The Pitt Building, Trumpington Street, Cambridge CB2 1RP
40 West 20th Street, New York, NY 10011–4211, USA
10 Stamford Road, Oakleigh, Melbourne 3166, Australia

First published 1994

Printed in Great Britain at the University Press, Cambridge

A catalogue record for this book is available from the British Library

Library of Congress cataloguing in publication data
Rushton, Julian.
Berlioz, Roméo et Juliette / Julian Rushton.
p. cm. – (Cambridge music handbooks)
Includes bibliographical references (p.   ) and index.
ISBN 0 521 37397 2 (hardback). – ISBN 0 521 37767 6 (paperback).
1. Berlioz, Hector, 1803–1869. Roméo et Juliette.
I. Title. II. Series.
ML410.B5R85 1994
784.2'2–dc20 93–32505 CIP MN

ISBN 0 521 37397 2 hardback
ISBN 0 521 37767 6 paperback

AH

Dedicated without permission but in heartfelt gratitude to the conductors whose live performances of 'Roméo et Juliette' ring in the memory:

Colin Davis
David Lloyd-Jones
Roger Norrington

et enfin permettez-moi de prononcer, puisque'il s'agit d'influence, le nom de mon auteur favori, pour moi du plus grand de tous les musiciens. Je veux parler de Hector Berlioz. Je suis un des rares musiciens français à reconnaître le plus grand musicien français, et à aimer Hector Berlioz, non seulement pour *La Damnation de Faust*, la *Symphonie fantastique*, mais pour son oeuvre le plus génial: je veux parler de *Roméo et Juliette*.

Olivier Messiaen

Contents

List of abbreviations and acknowledgements   *page* ix

1 Introduction   1

2 The genesis of *Roméo et Juliette*   7

3 Berlioz, Shakespeare, and Garrick   15

4 Exordium: *Introduction* and Prologue; *Roméo seul*   21

5 The heart of the matter: *Scène d'amour*; *La reine Mab*   35

6 Tragedy and reconciliation: *Convoi funèbre*;   47
   Roméo au tombeau; Finale

7 A view from 1839 by Stephen Heller   60

8 Performance and reception: 1839 and beyond   70

9 Afterword: *Roméo et Juliette* as covert opera   80

Appendix 1

   (a) Berlioz's Preface   87
   (b) Berlioz's note on *Roméo au tombeau des Capulets*   88
   (c) Berlioz's observations on performance   88
   (d) Berlioz on the 'genre *instrumental expressif*'   90

Contents

Appendix 2

Texts of:
(a) Prologue   91
(b) Finale   95
(c) The discarded Second Prologue   100

Notes   102

Select bibliography   115

Index   118

Abbreviations and acknowledgements

The following abbreviations are used in the notes (full details of publications are in the Select bibliography):

CG   *Correspondance générale de Hector Berlioz*: references are to the number of the letter cited followed by the volume and page number, thus *CG* 655 (II, p. 562).

Holoman, *Catalogue*   D. Kern Holoman, *Catalogue of the Works of Hector Berlioz*.

Mémoires   Berlioz, *Mémoires d'Hector Berlioz*: references are made to chapters so that the passage can be traced whichever edition is consulted.

Memoirs   D. Cairns (editor and translator), *The Memoirs of Hector Berlioz*.

NBE   New Berlioz Edition, general editor Hugh Macdonald (Kassel: Bärenreiter, 1969–): reference is made to individual volumes but *NBE* by itself refers to Vol. 18, *Roméo et Juliette*, edited by D. Kern Holoman (published 1990).

All translations are mine unless specifically acknowledged, but in rendering excerpts from Berlioz's *Mémoires* I acknowledge the universal debt to David Cairns's version.

    Like all Berliozians I depend heavily on the prior work of Hugh Macdonald and D. Kern Holoman, and I would like to express my personal indebtedness to them both. Ian Kemp kindly shared the material of his article before publication and provided me with a copy of the 1827 acting version of *Romeo and Juliet*: I apologize to him for disagreements expressed later on. I am grateful to Katharine Ellis and Leslie Horn for supplying copies of contemporary criticisms and to Katharine and Penny Souster for many helpful suggestions and for reading the script, since I could not objectively do so in my capacity as General Editor of Cambridge Music Handbooks. I am grateful to those who have listened to me on the subject of *Roméo et Juliette* and its tomb scene in conferences, lectures and classes in various countries; I have derived much benefit from the feedback. Remaining flaws and omissions are, of course, my own.

1

Introduction

In his preface to *Roméo et Juliette*, made available to its first audience in 1839 (see Appendix 1a), Berlioz insists that it is 'a symphony, and not a concert opera'.[1] The composer's view is of course to be respected, but need not end the argument. The seven movements of *Roméo et Juliette* resemble no previous symphony, not even the obvious, indeed only, precedent for a 'symphonie avec choeurs'. Beethoven's Ninth, perhaps unknown to Berlioz when he first conceived *Roméo*, has the usual four movements, and voices appear only in the finale, as an additional sonorous resource and as bearers of a verbal message. In his *Pastoral* symphony, Beethoven required five movements, the last three playing continuously. Berlioz has five in the programmatic *Symphonie fantastique*, but while the 'Marche au supplice' and 'Songe d'une nuit de Sabbat' constitute, dramatically, a dream sequence as against the virtual reality of the first three movements, each movement is fully cadenced. This, rather than any work of Beethoven, is the nearest precedent for *Roméo*; but it does not, of course, involve voices.

Berlioz's intentions are clear enough on at least one level. He aimed to use the language of 'expressive instrumental music' in order to present the essence of the play in a work for the concert hall rather than the theatre.[2] This choice, whether made out of aesthetic preference or because no other medium was available to him (see Chapter 2), enabled him to dispose instrumental and vocal forces freely in accordance with his preference for representing different aspects of the play in different ways: for instance, the lovers by instrumental music, the scene of reconciliation by music 'in the domain of opera or oratorio' (Preface, see Appendix 1a). The essential plot, for Berlioz, is that amid the fighting of two Veronese families, kept apart by the orders of the Prince, Romeo, a Montague, and Juliet, a Capulet, fall in love. They are married by Friar Lawrence who hopes thereby to reconcile the families. Strife resumes; Romeo kills Juliet's kinsman Tybalt and is exiled; Juliet is ordered to marry Count Paris. Lawrence produces a drug which makes her simulate death; she is buried. Through a tragic misunderstanding Romeo finds her apparently dead; entering her tomb, he takes poison; Juliet, awakening, stabs herself. The families resume their quarrel but Lawrence shames them into reconciliation.

Denuded of all minor characters, this is hardly an adequate representation of Shakespeare's play. In any case, only Lawrence, in Berlioz's version, has his own voice, even if others are represented in the orchestra. But what Berlioz required was an outline to be fleshed out, not in the richly accumulating detail of personalities and articulate speech, but in the inarticulate expressiveness of music's most sophisticated medium.[3] At the same time he believed in defining the limits within which the listener should experience his musical discourse: the auditor was expected to consider the particular dramatic circumstances which gave rise to the music. Yet no drama is to be enacted, and the movements do not follow a sequence which could convey, in a complete performance, the outline of the plot.

Reduced to generic types, the movements are (No. 1) a combative introduction and vocal Prologue, (No. 2) a scene of erotic meditation followed by a dance, (No. 3) a scene of nocturnal tenderness, (No. 4) a fleeting scherzo, (No. 5) a funeral procession with voices, (No. 6) a barely coherent, gestural scene of violent, conclusive action, and (No. 7) an operatic finale.[4] Even with movement titles, which I have temporarily suppressed, *Roméo et Juliette* does not follow a direct narrative pattern. Some of the story is outlined in the Prologue and (retrospectively) in Lawrence's narration during the finale, but its dramatic incidents are reduced to a minimum: nothing corresponds to such crucial stages in the argument as the lovers' marriage, the resumption of strife, the death of Tybalt, the second love-scene (Shakespeare's III.5), and Romeo's exile. Knowledge of these is assumed until Lawrence's narration, and nothing in the score corresponds to them; where they come in the play, Berlioz supplies only a scherzo, displaced from the location of its inspiration, the colourful speech by Mercutio which comes before the Ball scene. It appears, therefore, difficult to conceive *Roméo et Juliette* as a dramatic form, related to the play in a fashion analogous to an opera. Table 1.1 shows the natural order of events in relation to Shakespeare's play. Scenes not reflected in the symphony are omitted; the table includes the short movement titles, used hereafter.

Conceived as a symphony, *Roméo et Juliette* is scarcely less anomalous than when it is considered as a dramatic form. Auguste Morel, an early commentator close to Berlioz, suggested that the second, third, fourth, and seventh sections could be regarded as analogous to Beethoven's Ninth, but this leaves a large proportion of the work out of account.[5] Of the seven movements of its final form, the first is composite, and the last Berlioz admitted to be in the nature of an operatic finale. The original plan included a second Prologue, placed after the scherzo or, more pertinently, before the *Convoi funèbre*. The

Table 1.1 Comparison of the play and the symphony

Play	Symphony
Act I	No. 1 *Combats, tumulte . . .*
Prologue	Strife, intervention of the Prince
Strife, intervention of the Prince	Prologue
Romeo and friends	No. 2 *Roméo seul*
Mercutio's Queen Mab speech	
Ball at Capulet's	*Grande fête chez Capulet*
Act II Garden. Love-scene	No. 3 *Scène d'amour*
The marriage	
	No. 4 *La reine Mab* (Scherzo)
Act III Death of Mercutio,	
Romeo kills Tybalt and is	
banished. Love-scene in	
Juliet's room. Juliet betrothed	
to Paris.	
Act IV Juliet takes potion and	No. 5 *Convoi funèbre de Juliette*
appears dead.	
Act V Romeo to the tomb,	No. 6 *Roméo au tombeau*
kills Paris, takes poison, dies.	Romeo takes poison.
	Juliet awakens, brief reunion, Romeo
Juliet awakens, stabs herself, dies.	dies, Juliet stabs herself, dies.
Lawrence's narration	No. 7 Lawrence's narration
Prince forces reconciliation.	Lawrence forces reconciliation.

grouping this implies – four movements followed by three – is still apparent in the definitive form; the symphony, from dramatic and musical points of view, divides sharply after No. 4. Up to this point the scene has been set and the love of Romeo and Juliet explored; the last three movements tend to the tragic dénouement and the culminating reconciliation of the warring families. Berlioz, indeed, suggested an intermission after the scherzo (see Appendix 1c).

Given the weight of Berlioz's finale, it appears that the theme of reconciliation was fundamental to his conception. Yet there is no doubt that most people in the nineteenth century would have considered the death of the lovers

3

to be the real ending, and many performances of *Romeo and Juliet* ended there, thus falling in with a tendency in nineteenth-century theatre – in line with contemporary operatic tendencies – away from a governing theme and towards concentration on the fate of individuals. Many plots, of course, are designed to complement the closure of the public action with the death of one or more protagonists (*La Juive, Les Huguenots, Aida*). In *La Damnation de Faust* and *Les Troyens* Berlioz only partly conforms to this tendency, for in both he brings a wider issue – the fate of the Trojans, the mysteries of salvation and damnation – to the fore; the transfiguration of Marguerite hints at the possible future redemption of Faust himself, while Dido dies with a vision of the future splendour of Rome.[6] This impulse towards elevating the general over the particular is still stronger in Berlioz's 'Dramatic Symphony'. Rather than viewing it as a series of beautiful or strange scenes (Nos. 2 to 6) within a more or less unsatisfactory frame (Nos. 1 and 7), we should consider the frame (the strife and reconciliation of the families) as of equal importance to the scenes within.

The public conflict and reconciliation which begin and end the work are the principal dramatic theme, symbolized by the transformation of the opening fugato as an operatic quarrel with voices. Shakespeare's prologues go some way towards justification of Berlioz's strategy. The first, before Act I, epitomizes the drama:

> Two households, both alike in dignity,
> In fair Verona, where we lay our scene,
> From ancient grudge break to new mutiny,
> Where civil blood makes civil hands unclean.
> From forth the fatal loins of these two foes
> A pair of star-cross'd lovers take their life . . .

Only one line concerns the title-roles directly; the primary theme of the play is the evil of faction and the virtue of reconciliation.[7] The tonal departure of Berlioz's No. 1 from its opening key of B minor to tonal areas associated with later instrumental sections corresponds to a shift in dramatic concentration from public conflict to the private domains of eroticism, love, and dreams. The ball scene embodies open domestic harmony with no more than a rumbling of discontent, and the funeral procession is undisturbed by strife; the apparent death of Juliet is not attributed to any act of the Montagues. In Nos. 3 and 5 voices reappear in lyrical, then elegiac vein, and in the style of an opera, although no named characters appear until the finale. Berlioz's consistent policy is to represent the lovers' tragedy by instrumental music; hence the tomb scene, despite being representational in its essence, terminates the

4

symphonic part of the scheme. Finally, the primary theme proposed as strife in the Introduction is recovered and complemented by the overtly dramatic finale and its scenes of renewed strife and reconciliation.

This point is emphasized by a broad tonal structure. That Berlioz begins and ends in the same key, or at least with the same tonic (the introduction in B minor and the oath of reconciliation in B major) might seem unworthy of comment, since symphonies before Mahler hardly ever behaved otherwise; they are designated by their keys for just this reason.[8] But given that the symphonic heart of *Roméo* is generally agreed to be the three movements in F, A, and F (No. 2, introduction and allegro; No. 3, slow movement; No. 4, scherzo), followed by movements in E and A (Nos. 5 and 6), the framing key of B appears alien; indeed, the central keys are only feasible because the Prologue ends, and the finale begins, in keys other than B (see Table 1.2).

Tonal 'unity', therefore, is not an issue in this symphony, and it plays no role in my analysis (Chapters 4–6). But the over-arching tonal connection is delineated by an audible cross-reference, like an operatic reminiscence: the opening of the introduction, a brusque fugato in B minor, reappears in the finale at the moment which re-establishes B as a tonal centre. This event (No. 7, bar 240) coincides with a coming together of divergent musical forces. The fugato introduction is headed 'Combats, tumulte', and the brief reworking of this section in the finale is a declaration of continuing hatred between the warring families, to the words 'But our blood reddens their swords; and ours rises up against them. Villains! no peace! Cowards, no mercy!', interspersed with a catalogue of the dead. Instrumental and vocal music combine; the instrumental fugato is sung, and Berlioz's means of expression find a measure of reconciliation, although in a context which threatens to overwhelm the pleas of Friar Lawrence.

A major theme of the critical reception of *Roméo et Juliette*, even into the present century (see Chapter 8), at least when performances were rare and recordings non-existent, has been to deplore the overall design and regard with some scepticism the choral movements and *Roméo au tombeau*, while professing warm admiration for the first three instrumental movements (Nos. 2–4), which are frequently extracted to form a concert suite. The problem is one of genre: of a framework within which the work can be 'understood'. There has been some reluctance to accept that a work may be *sui generis*, generically mixed but nevertheless satisfying on its own terms, and Berlioz's own symphonic claim does not help. For there was no symphony like it in 1839, nor has it started a tradition. In Chapter 9 I explore the view that *Roméo et Juliette* should not be regarded primarily as a symphony. Not only are its

Table 1.2 Tonal outline of *Roméo et Juliette*

No. 1	Introduction: combats	B minor [D–V/b]
	Intervention	various: ends V/b
	Prologue	from V/b: various
	Ball music	A–F
	Romeo sighs	D
	Love music	E
	Strophes	G
	Scherzetto	F
	Tragic foreboding	A minor
No. 2	*Roméo seul: Tristesse:* *Grande fête chez Capulet*	F major
No. 3	*Scène d'amour*	A
No. 4	Scherzo	F
No. 5	*Convoi funèbre*	E minor[i]
No. 6	*Roméo au tombeau*	E minor, C sharp minor
	Reunion and death of the lovers	A major
No. 7	Families enter	A minor
	Lawrence's narration	C minor
	Aria (Larghetto)	E flat major
		(Allegro) B major
	Strife resumes	B minor (to V/D)
	Lawrence's response	D/B minor: B major
	Oath of reconciliation	B major[ii]

i No. 5 ends in the minor despite its final key-signature of E major.
ii No. 1 (B minor to A minor) and No. 7 (A minor to B) are 'palindromic', but this is hardly audible, and the end of No. 1 is qualified by the chiming of the pitch E which anticipates the E minor of No. 5.

overtly symphonic elements qualified (as in the *Symphonie fantastique*) by demonstrably programmatic intentions; its anti-symphonic elements are indispensable to a conception which in a curious and perhaps unique way fulfils the implications of the generic term Berlioz explicitly rejected: 'concert opera'.

The genesis of Roméo et Juliette

From 1827: inspiration

The 'supreme drama' of his life has never been better told than by Berlioz himself.[1] It occurred during the 1827 Shakespeare season given in Paris by a British troupe, a season which made an enduring impression on all French Romantics (see Chapter 3); but even the poets and playwrights were not more profoundly affected than the composer, who wrote: 'I saw Harriet Smithson, whom I married five years later, playing Ophelia. The impression her outstanding talent, indeed her dramatic genius, made on my heart and mind, is only comparable to the upset which I suffered from the poet whose worthy interpreter she was. I can say no more.' He nevertheless describes his perturbation of mind and body, then, his sense of irony reviving, continues:

When I came out after the performance of *Hamlet*, terrified by what I had experienced, I solemnly swore not to expose myself for a second time to the Shakespearean fire.

Next day they announced *Romeo and Juliet* . . . I had my pass to the Odéon pit; so, afraid new instructions might be given to the porter which would stop me getting in the usual way, as soon as I saw the announcement for this drama, I made doubly sure of my place by rushing to the box office to buy a stall. [. . .].[2]

After the melancholy, the heart-rending suffering [. . .], after the icy winds of Denmark, to bask in the ardent sunshine and balmy Italian night, to watch the growth of this love, swift as thought, boiling like lava, imperious, irresistible, immense yet chaste and lovely as an angel's smile, those furious scenes of revenge, those desperate embraces, the despairing struggles of love and death, were all too much. So by Act III, scarcely breathing, suffering as if an iron fist were clutching my heart, I told myself with perfect certainty: I am lost! – I must add that I knew not a word of English at the time, that I only glimpsed Shakespeare through the fog of Letourneur's translation, and therefore I saw nothing of the poetic thread whose golden tracery enfolds his marvellous ideas.[3] [. . .] But the acting, especially that of the actress, the succession of scenes, the gestures and vocal inflections, meant more to me and were a thousand times more effective than the words of this bland and inaccurate translation in penetrating me with Shakespearean ideas and passions. An English critic last winter wrote in the *Illustrated London News* that after seeing Miss Smithson play Juliet I exclaimed: 'I shall marry this woman! and I shall base my greatest symphony on this play!'[4] I did it, but I said no such thing; my biographer ascribed to me an ambition larger than life.

Although the London journalist is unlikely to have scented such specific smoke without any fire at all, we may never know when Berlioz first considered using the play as the basis of a symphony, particularly as some of his early thoughts tended in the direction of a *Romeo and Juliet* opera. But there is also evidence that the form of *Roméo et Juliette* was not merely a response to his rejection by the operatic establishment after the failure of *Benvenuto Cellini* in 1838, and that a symphonic conception may date back ten years or more, before its completion in 1839, to a period not long after his first encounter with Shakespeare.

One pointer to this is Berlioz's encounter with Beethoven, described in Chapter 20 of his Memoirs in connection with the opening of the Société des Concerts du Conservatoire conducted by Habeneck, on 23 March 1828. The first concert included the *Eroica* symphony. However, Berlioz had almost certainly become acquainted with Beethoven before then. His first two symphonies were in the repertoire of the Concert spirituel;[5] and Berlioz may have heard something during Habeneck's notoriously prolonged rehearsal periods. He was in Italy at the time of the first Paris performance of the Ninth, but he had certainly read the score before discussing the work in his first articles on Beethoven, published in 1829.[6]

The general influence of Beethoven is well expressed by David Cairns: Berlioz 'grasped at once that the symphony . . . was a dramatic form. The effect of the Conservatoire concerts was not to shake his allegiance to dramatic music but to widen his whole concept of it to include the symphonic.'[7] It was surely Beethoven who led Berlioz to his view that 'instrumental language' could in certain cases be 'richer, more varied, less inhibited and, by its very indefiniteness, incomparably more powerful' than vocal music (preface to *Roméo et Juliette*; see Appendix 1a). The first practical manifestation of this enthusiasm may have been a revision of the 1826 overture *Les Francs-juges*.[8] In 1830, he completed the *Symphonie fantastique*: the crystallization of its conception displaced ideas for 'a descriptive symphony on *Faust*' contemplated early in 1829.[9]

Given Berlioz's lateral mode of thought, it is not surprising that he associated Shakespeare with Goethe's drama, just as he later used lines from *The Merchant of Venice* for the love-duet in *Les Troyens*. In April 1829 Berlioz published his Goethe settings, *Huit scènes de Faust*. Each movement in the

8

work he proudly labelled 'Oeuvre I' bears a Shakespeare epigraph in English: five are from *Hamlet*, the rest from *Romeo and Juliet*. This was an implicit manifesto of the profound rapport he considered to exist among the truly great, and the choice of epigraphs is significant for the later symphony. No. 2 of the *Huit scènes* ('Paysans sous les tilleuls') is a brisk, rather lewd dance; the epigraph is from the ball scene: 'Capulet: Who'll now deny to dance? She that makes dainty, I'll swear hath corns' (I.5). No. 3 is the seductive, dreamlike *Concert de Sylphes*, preceded by 'Mercutio: I talk of dreams, which are the children of an airy brain, begot of nothing but vain fantasy; which is as thin of substance as the air, and more inconstant than the wind.' These words follow the Queen Mab speech (I.4), inspiration for Berlioz's equally seductive and dreamlike scherzo. No. 7, Marguerite's Romance, is preceded by 'Romeo: Ay me, sad hours seem long' (I.1). Almost his first words, this phrase is clearly part of the inspiration for Berlioz's own invention, the erotic meditation *Roméo seul*.

These details, as well as the *Mémoires*, make it clear that Harriet and *Romeo and Juliet* remained in Berlioz's thoughts well after 1827. Berlioz's eventual librettist Emile Deschamps claimed in 1844 that the composer had approached him about words for the symphony ten years before its completion. This is often assumed to refer to the period of the first impact of Shakespeare (1827), twelve years before; but it is more likely that Deschamps meant 1829, a year in which, having by now absorbed a great deal of Beethoven, Berlioz might well have been thinking of a symphony.[10] Yet Deschamps' memory may have been affected by the actual composition of the symphony in the meantime; the possibility should not be ruled out that what he originally discussed with Berlioz was an opera. During his period as Prix de Rome laureate in Italy (1831–2), Berlioz was still preoccupied with the play. When he saw it in Florence, he included Bellini's *Romeo and Juliet* opera, *I Capuleti e i Montecchi*, among the calamities of modern Italian culture; prejudice concealed its excellent qualities. He hated hearing a woman sing Romeo, and, unaware that Romani's libretto used sources other than Shakespeare, he could not understand its organization: 'no ball at Capulet's, no Mercutio, no chattering nurse, no grave and serene hermit, no balcony scene, no sublime soliloquy for Juliet as she takes the hermit's drug, no duet in the cell between the banished Romeo and the distressed friar, no Shakespeare, nothing – a botched piece of work'.

He offers a more accurate catalogue of the contents of the future symphony a little earlier, as he affects to recall his excited anticipation of the Bellini opera:

9

What a subject! How well made for music! First the glittering ball at Capulet's, where, among the busy swarm of beauties, young Montague first sees *sweet Juliet*, whose fidelity will cost her life; then the ferocious street-fighting in Verona, with Tybalt simmering over it like the genius of anger and revenge; the incomparable nocturne on Juliet's balcony, where the lovers murmur their concord of love tenderly, softly, chastely, like the friendly watching moonbeams; then insouciant Mercutio and his sharp-witted buffoonery; the simple chatter of the old nurse; the solemn character of the hermit, vainly seeking to impose calm upon the flood of love and hatred which even penetrates his cell . . . then the terrible catastrophe, ecstasy of happiness struggling with that of despair, loving sighs turning into a death-rattle, and finally the solemn oath of the warring families, swearing, too late, on the bodies of their unhappy children, to extinguish the hatred which shed so much blood, so many tears.[11]

But these comments refer explicitly to *Romeo and Juliet* as an opera. Auguste Barbier says that Berlioz, in Rome in 1832, asked him for a *Romeo and Juliet* libretto; probably an opera was again in question, for a Prix de Rome winner could expect an invitation to write one on his return to Paris.[12] Nevertheless, in conversation with Mendelssohn Berlioz let slip a clue to what may have been a latent symphonic intention:

It was on one of my riding trips in the Roman Campagna with Felix Mendelssohn that I expressed surprise that no one had yet thought of writing a *scherzo* on Shakespeare's sparkling little poem *Queen Mab*. He showed equal surprise, and I repented at once having given him the idea. For many years after I was afraid of hearing that he had used this subject. He would certainly have made impossible, or at least decidedly rash, the double attempt that I made in my symphony *Roméo et Juliette*. Luckily for me he did not think of it.[13]

Early in 1833, Berlioz's enthusiastic anticipation of again seeing Harriet as Juliet led him to babble, in pseudo-Shakespearean English, in a letter to Albert Du Boys: 'I am mad, dearest I am dead!! Sweetest juliet! my life, my soul, my heart, all, all, t'is the heaven oh!!!!! . . . parle donc, mon orchestre'.[14] The final words in French remind us of an association between Harriet and a symphonic ideal already apparent from the *Symphonie fantastique*.

First musical ideas

In 1829, the year of his original discussion with Deschamps, Berlioz composed, in addition to the *Huit scènes de Faust*, two other pieces which are related to his Shakespeare symphony. Composed some time between April and December, *Le Ballet des ombres*, a chorus with text by Du Boys, is the source of the theme for the antique-cymbal episode in *La reine Mab* (see below,

Chapter 4, p. 45).[15] In July, writing his annual competition cantata for the Prix de Rome, and despite the banalities of the libretto (by one Vieillard), Berlioz was deeply moved by the plight of Cleopatra; when she imagines herself entombed with her ancestors Berlioz associated the music with Juliet, writing to Humbert Ferrand: 'It's terrifying, horrific; it's the scene where Juliet meditates on her entombment in the Capulet mausoleum, alive and surrounded by the bones of her ancestors, the body of Tybalt . . .'.[16] The allusion is to IV.3, the monologue 'Farewell! God knows when we shall meet again' and particularly the line 'How if, when I am laid into the tomb', which is inscribed in the autograph score of *Cléopâtre*. Whether Berlioz had already conceived this sombre music in connection with Juliet and used it under examination pressure for Cleopatra in an analogous situation, or whether he recalled Shakespeare to generate inspiration in his task, one cannot say. The powerful harmony and unorthodox rhythm inspired by the idea of living entombment did more than anything, even its starkly verismo close, to deprive Berlioz of the prize which he was universally expected to win.[17] But when Berlioz re-used the music, it was as No. 2 ('Chorus of angry shades'), in *Le Retour à la vie* (1831), later retitled *Lélio*, where the immediate context is not *Romeo and Juliet* but an invocation of the ghost's speech in *Hamlet*.[18]

A closer association exists between *Roméo* and the Prix de Rome cantata of July 1830, *Sardanapale*. This time Berlioz won, he claimed, by being deliberately conventional: 'Both of them [the judges], having recognized, thanks to a piece I have since burned, my conversion to doctrinal health, they at last, at last, at last, awarded me first prize.'[19] He nevertheless included the cantata in concerts of the early 1830s, and its eventual destruction does not mean that he despised it more than earlier cantatas which have survived.[20] But as with *Cléopâtre*, he had other uses for the music. The surviving fragment of *Sardanapale* includes two themes which reappear in *Roméo* No. 2: the lyrical oboe theme and the main theme of the dance (see Chapter 4).[21] Again, there is no knowing if they occurred to him first in connection with *Roméo et Juliette* or if he first thought of them while closeted in the Institute to write his cantata; but the working habits revealed by other cases of self-borrowing suggest the former hypothesis is no less likely than the latter.[22]

D. Kern Holoman remarks that '*Roméo et Juliette* is, on the one hand, the jewel of the golden decade; it remained, on the other, a work in progress for most of Berlioz's active life'.[23] Begun in imagination in 1827 or at the latest 1829, it reached its final form only with the publication of a second edition of the full score in 1857, followed by a vocal score in 1858.[24] Much the same, of course, can be said of other Berlioz works; from reading *Faust* to the first publication of *La Damnation* took twenty-seven years, while the seeds of *Les Troyens* were sown in readings of Virgil under the tutelage of his father, before Berlioz left his native Côte-St-André. Nevertheless *Roméo*, as Holoman says, is emphatically the culminating work of the 'golden' 1830s, a decade dominated by the experience of Italy and marriage to Harriet. After the completion and performance of the *Symphonie fantastique* and his first Shakespearean work, the fantasy-overture *The Tempest*, Berlioz spent a turbulent period in Italy during which he suffered sexual betrayal (the ending of his engagement to Camille Moke),[25] serious *ennui* (he found the musical and cultural life of Italy insufferable), and a drying-up of musical inventiveness. While there he composed little, and that not on Italian themes. But the scenery and sky haunted his memory; many of his later works have Italian references.[26]

Back from Italy, Berlioz embodied his experiences of the colour of Italian life and his own isolation in the picturesque symphony with solo viola, *Harold en Italie*. Something of his feeling for the political and artistic establishment emerges in the opera *Benvenuto Cellini*, begun in 1834 and finally performed, to a poor critical and public reception, at the Paris Opéra in September 1838. Disillusioned by his encounter with the opera performers and management while still (as far as one can tell) happily married to his Ophelia/Juliet, Berlioz may have returned spontaneously to the idea of a symphony on the second play in which he had seen Harriet perform (a treatment for which *Hamlet*, perhaps, was hardly suitable).

Composition: 1838–9

Whether he would have written it without the intervention of Paganini is doubtful. At Berlioz's concert on 16 December 1838 the programme included *Harold*, the work originally intended as a symphonic viola concerto for the great virtuoso. Afterwards Paganini, his throat ravaged by disease and speaking through his son, told Berlioz that he had never been so moved by a concert: 'He is overcome by your music, and he is preventing himself with difficulty from kneeling down to thank you.'[27] Hearing *Harold* may have touched Paganini's conscience as well as his sense of beauty; and any minor slight to Berlioz (whose talent was hardly fitted, as he himself remarked, for concerto-writing) is more than redeemed by this public gesture and its sequel, recorded in a short letter in Italian:

My dear friend, Beethoven being dead, only Berlioz remains to make him live again; and I who have relished your divine compositions, worthy of the genius that you are, think it my duty to ask you to accept, in token of my homage, twenty thousand francs, which Baron de Rothschild will pay over when you present him the enclosed. Believe me, I am ever your most affectionate friend, Niccolò Paganini.[28]

One might infer from his *Mémoires* that Berlioz virtually abandoned regular journalism while he concentrated on his symphony. In fact he only slightly reduced his output during 1839, writing over thirty articles; but Paganini's gift enabled him to pay several debts and so granted him the security, and the confidence, to tackle a huge undertaking and risk the outlay of mounting three performances in the closing days of 1839.[29] 'What a life of passion I lived during all that time! With what energy I swam forth on that great sea of poetry, caressed by the intoxicating winds of fantasy . . .'. Thus Berlioz recalled the happy months during which composition of *Roméo* was his chief preoccupation. He confided to Ferrand his intention to honour Paganini with a symphony on 2 January 1839, although he said a period of indecision had preceded the choice of subject.[30] Formal work on the music began on 24 January, despite the death nine days earlier of his young brother Prosper.

By this time he must have made his prose draft of the necessary texts, which he conveyed to Deschamps. He began composing with No. 2; inspiration pressed too hard for him to wait for the poet to supply the Prologue.[31] He reached the end on 8 September, a date noted on both the finale and (perhaps suggesting it was finished last) on No. 6, *Roméo au tombeau*; he had found the finale and the love-scene particularly difficult to compose. And this, of course, was not the end of the compositional process but the point at which he could safely plan the first performance. Changes (some in the light of friendly criticism and experience: see Chapters 7–8) were made before the second and third performances in 1839, others before publication in 1847; very few changes were required for the second edition in 1857. Berlioz's practice of performing and revising a work before publication means that no doubt remains concerning the definitive text. Berlioz's autograph, although a fascinating document, approximates in its final reading quite closely to his last and published thoughts, and it was his habit at least partly to obliterate earlier versions; we simply do not have, therefore, all the music which was performed in 1839.

The first three performances took place on 24 November, 1 December, and 15 December. All intellectual Paris was interested; reporting 'a great success' to his father, Berlioz quoted Balzac: 'your concert hall is a *brain*', and an early critic noted that the audience was worthy of the revelation of a novel and magnificent conception based on Shakespeare: 'Eminent men, celebrated artists, princes, learned men, young people devoted to the study of music, women distinguished by intelligence or [*sic*] beauty, an illustrious public, an intelligent public'.[32] Berlioz's preparations were of unprecedented thoroughness. Unlike his recent major premières, the Requiem and *Benvenuto Cellini*, this was his own promotion, so he himself conducted the 200 performers, insisting on sectional rehearsals, then something of a novelty. In the Prologue Alexis Dupont, who had sung Cellini, was the tenor solo, Emily Widemann the contralto; Berlioz was particularly pleased with Louis Alizard as Friar Lawrence. The Conservatoire hall, for whose excellent acoustic Berlioz conceived much of his symphonic music, was well filled, and the receipts of three performances amounted to 13,200 francs. Doubtless this bold undertaking, of presenting the work three times, was intended in the fashion of a run of opera performances to recoup the enormous expenses of copying.[33] But the musicians, publicity, and the hire of the hall cost more than for a single performance. At the time Berlioz reckoned his expenses at 12,000 francs, and several months later he told his sister Nanci that the performances had actually lost 1600 francs: 'c'est la grande musique qui me ruine'.[34] Nowadays, counting Paganini's 20,000 francs as sponsorship, he would be considered to have made a handsome profit. And although he quickly recognized that the work had faults, at the time he was rightly proud of what he had achieved. At one performance the audience included Richard Wagner, though the significance of this would not be clear for some years.[35] Conceived at the beginning of the French Romantic decade, *Roméo et Juliette* was composed and performed near its end to a receptive audience and largely appreciative critics (see Chapters 7–8). In every respect except financially, it was a triumph, perhaps the greatest of Berlioz's chequered career.

3

Berlioz, Shakespeare, and Garrick

When Berlioz arrived to study medicine in Paris in 1821, the French cultural establishment was dominated by a neo-classical, post-Racine tradition which had endured since the seventeenth century. Berlioz was brought up on a classical diet; yet it is clear from his account of reading Virgil that he valued artistic works for their emotional truth rather than for those austere, architectural qualities which we tend to associate with neo-classicism.[1] And passion, of course, was what he later found in his first musical hero, Gluck, whose *Iphigénie* operas (both based on neo-classical French plays) he adored. He recognized in true classicism a rhetorical framework for the ordering of experience which never precludes powerful, indeed harrowing emotions. In his Stendhal-like article of 1832 he called music which (in his view) merely filled up a form with ideas 'classical'.[2] Thus he was predisposed to favour works which, like Beethoven's symphonies rather than those of Haydn and Mozart, were 'romantic' in that the idea determined the form.

The language of 'expressive instrumental music' was revealed to Berlioz by Beethoven, but he was if anything still more susceptible to literature; he enthusiastically accepted the Romantic vogue for Goethe, Schiller, Scott, and Byron, whose works became a quarry for literary, visual, and musical inspiration. The influence of Shakespeare was incomparably greater than these, and still more emblematic of rebellion because, until 1827, he had been condescended to by French cultural orthodoxy as an inspired barbarian whose works needed severe revision to become palatable. Shakespeare's true value was appreciated only when his works were given in English, even though the 1827 audience could scarcely grasp their poetic beauty. Hence for our purposes what may be important is the Shakespeare Berlioz *saw*: the outline plot, represented in scene and gesture. It is surely significant that the plays were presented expensively, with realistic scenery and (for the period) acting; the effect on *Roméo et Juliette* of the visible unfolding of the drama should not be underestimated.[3]

Shakespeare was promptly adopted by the Romantic movement in general,

15

but his works were already available in print, both in English and in French translations.[4] In fact, the 1827 season was not the introduction of even semi-authentic Shakespeare to France; some performances by an English company in 1822 had passed almost without effect on the public, although artists such as Hugo and Delacroix probably attended them. Some of the intelligentsia had already noticed that the British barbarian was not Voltaire's 'ape of genius'. Berlioz's fellow Dauphinois Stendhal claimed Racine and Shakespeare for Romanticism but considered Shakespeare the more truly romantic, for he laid bare the secrets of the human heart – a phrase unconsciously echoed by Berlioz.[5] A good part of the impact of the 1827 season was due to Harriet Smithson; yet she took the leading female roles of Ophelia, Juliet, Desdemona, and Jane Shore by the unexpected circumstance of a better-known actress being unavailable. She made the most of her opportunity, and this was the high point of an otherwise relatively undistinguished and cruelly abbreviated career. To understand her triumph it is necessary to recall that the all-seeing, all-powerful director did not yet exist; the plays were mounted under the direction of the actor/manager (here Charles Kemble), but individuals could to a great extent work out their own interpretations. Harriet's passionate involvement contrasted markedly with the cooler, more coquettish Juliet of Miss Foote.[6]

Writing under the impact of the 1822 performances, Stendhal urged Romantic drama to defy the classical unities, a prescription also urged by Victor Hugo in the preface to *Cromwell* (1827) and put into practice two years later by Alexandre Dumas in *Henri III et sa cour*.[7] The 1827 Shakespeare revolution was the climax of a movement, not its inception. Delacroix began thirty years of occasional Shakespeare illustration as early as 1820, with a sketch of the farewell of Romeo and Juliet.[8] Nevertheless it was the 1827 performances which had a wide impact and led many to question the basis of neo-classical drama and by extension other aspects of French cultural life. Writers were naturally quick to react to the new vogue. The response of Dumas, Sainte-Beuve, Gautier and others to the Shakespeare season was less personal than Berlioz's but artistically of comparable significance; in the preface to *Cromwell* Hugo acclaimed Shakespeare as 'the sovereign poet', while some of Berlioz's friends engaged in the obvious literary response, translation. In 1826–7 Emile Deschamps, eventually Berlioz's librettist, collaborated with Alfred de Vigny in a translation of *Romeo and Juliet* intended for the Comédie française. It was not performed, but Vigny's *Othello* reached that illustrious stage in 1829. Deschamps eventually completed the translation and published it, together with the symphony's libretto, in 1844.[9]

More important was the liberating effect Shakespeare's drama had on the acceptable forms of the French stage. The Opéra, to its credit, accepted such Romantic, even politically subversive, works as *La Muette de Portici* in 1828 and *Guillaume Tell* in 1829. In the legitimate theatre, the Comédie française fell to Victor Hugo with *Hernani* in 1830, the year also of Berlioz's *Symphonie fantastique* and the political revolution for which most Romantic artists longed. This ended the restored Bourbon monarchy, essentially a throwback to the pre-1789 *ancien régime* (it led only to the bourgeois monarchy of Louis-Philippe, but memories of the July days remained to inspire the revolution of 1848). By 1839, in short, Romanticism had taken over the artistic establishment in France, and in acclaiming Berlioz's Shakespeare symphony the audience was, as so often, also applauding itself.

The obvious musical response to Shakespeare is to adapt his works, with all the inevitable fudges and compromises, as opera librettos.[10] Rossini's *Otello* had been performed in Paris as early as 1821, but only the final act is really near to Shakespeare's version. In his much later study of *Romeo and Juliet* operas, Berlioz praised that by Daniel Steibelt, performed in 1793 in Paris.[11] By the 1820s British subjects were generally in vogue and it is surprising that there were not more Shakespearean operas around 1830 (the year of Bellini's *I Capuleti e i Montecchi*), even in France.

The operatic avenue was closed to Berlioz, whose one Shakespearean opera, *Béatrice et Bénédict*, was conceived in the 1830s but not written until 1862. As a beginner of somewhat doubtful reputation, he was not invited to compose for any of the musical theatres. By 1827 he had already considered several operatic projects and finished one, *Les Francs-juges*.[12] In 1828 he turned his attention to *Faust*, contemplating a ballet and a symphony and setting several lyric scenes, valuable experience for operatic composition but not the real thing. Hence his Shakespearean passion found its first and principal outlet in a sphere with which, among French composers, Berlioz was to be particularly associated: the concert-hall, in which by 1839 he had already presented instrumental and vocal compositions over twelve years. In 1830 he performed a vibrant fantasy-overture, in reality a symphonic poem, on *The Tempest*.[13] After his visit to Italy he revived the *Symphonie fantastique* on 9 December 1832 with its new sequel *Le Retour à la vie*, piquantly in the presence of Harriet Smithson; 'tout Paris' knew by then whom the 'idée fixe' represented. The finest music Berlioz composed in Italy was the overture *King Lear*. Back in Paris, the chance to write an opera eventually came, resulting in nothing Shakespearean, although *Benvenuto Cellini*, like *Romeo and Juliet*, is an Italian Renaissance subject. But *Benvenuto* was not successful; the public Berlioz had cultivated in the concert-room was not that which sustained the Opéra. It was therefore natural that on gaining time and peace of mind thanks to Paganini, he should turn his attention to making, for presentation in the concert-hall, a monument to Shakespeare and incidentally a tribute to his own wife and to Beethoven.

Garrick and other versions

Versions of Shakespeare given in the theatre were usually far from authentic. Abbreviation, bowdlerization (even *avant la lettre*), and rewriting were endemic; long before Garrick there were Dryden, Shadwell, and in France, bowing to national taste, Voltaire. Compared to these, the versions by David Garrick (1717–79) are relatively faithful, retaining not only most of Shakespeare's verse but also his dramaturgy of multiple scenes and multiple characterizations while clearing away 'the Jingle and the Quibble which were always thought a great Objection to performing it'.[14] Garrick made a number of structural changes in *Romeo and Juliet*, involving the composition of some new verses, but most of his alterations are cuts and light adaptations which preserve the robust Elizabethan character of the verse; there is no attempt to make Shakespeare Augustan. Salient features of Garrick's version appear in the most widely read French translation, that of Letourneur, which Berlioz knew.[15] However, it is apparent from contemporary descriptions and from the French text sold at the door of the theatre that further cuts were observed in the 'Kemble version' used in the 1827 performances, among them Act I scene 2 (between Montague and Benvolio); II.1 (Benvolio and Mercutio); II.6 (the marriage scene); V.1 (the dirge); V.3; and the final scene.[16] This considerably weakens the sense of a society within which the individual tragedies unfold; steps were taken to compensate for this in the symphony.

Nevertheless the play performed in 1827 remains essentially Shakespeare's creation. In what follows, Garrick's principal alterations are detailed. Where the 'Kemble' version is not mentioned it is assumed to follow Garrick. In designing the symphony, however, Berlioz and Deschamps went back to Garrick's full text and beyond it to Shakespeare himself; they were far from dependent on memories of the 1827 production.

(1) Garrick removed the 'blemish in his character' of Romeo being in love with Rosaline before Juliet.[17] In Shakespeare his intention in going to Capulet's ball was to see Rosaline; Garrick has him sighing 'Oh Juliet, Juliet' almost as soon as he appears. The only effect on Berlioz's symphony is to provide an excuse to build on the words of Montague and Benvolio (I.2,

omitted in Kemble) and invent a passage called 'Romeo alone' (the opening of No. 2), an erotic meditation which by inference concerns Juliet.

(2) At the opening of Act V Garrick inserted a funeral procession for Juliet with a sung dirge ('Rise, rise: Heart-breaking sighs, The woe-fraught bosom swell; For sighs alone, And dismal moan, Should echo Juliet's knell'). This is clearly the origin of Berlioz's No. 5, although the words are quite different, taking off from Paris's lament before the tomb: 'Sweet flower, with flowers thy bridal bed I strew': 'Jetez des fleurs pour la vierge expirée'. But this dirge, probably because of the cost of the necessary musical elaboration, is not included in the Kemble version. As an excuse for a musical and processional interlude within the play, it is eminently operatic, and must have seemed, when Berlioz read Garrick's version, too good to leave out. Deschamps retained the scene, with different words, in his translation of the play.

(3) Most significantly, Garrick composed several new lines in a development of the tomb scene to include a final meeting of the doomed lovers. This scene of love-death was recognized as the most important of the drama; it is depicted in the 1750 publication of Garrick's adaptation. In Shakespeare, Romeo poisons himself and blesses the speed of the venom; he dies. Only then does Juliet stir, and after conversing with Friar Lawrence she takes the opportunity of his hastening away to stab herself; there is thus no lovers' dialogue. Garrick (his V.5) gave an additional turn to the tragic screw by having Juliet wake up while Romeo, having drunk poison, is still conscious. Her apparent return to life causes him to forget his condition, but after a moment of joyous reunion, he dies. Refusing to follow the friar, Juliet stabs herself.[18] The Kemble version ends here.

This major alteration to the death-scene, which, as Garrick noted, restores the plot of Shakespeare's source, was much admired. Berlioz was to admit without embarrassment to preferring Garrick's dénouement, unlike almost every other attempt to 'improve' a great original; he was in no position to realize the poverty, even silliness, of Garrick's verses although, through his sensitive ears, he seems to have felt the beauty of Shakespeare's poetry in, for instance, the love-scenes. Deschamps called the Garrick ending 'more gripping, more pathetic, more visually striking, by its alternations of ecstasy and despair . . . above all, it is more favourable to the movement and expression of the actors, a consideration which alone suffices to make it preferable. No other tragedy ends with such a catastrophe where pity and terror are carried to such an extreme. It goes to the point where spoken words are no longer enough for such a situation; one in which music, the language of emotion and sorrow, carries off the palm in opera [drame lyrique].'[19]

Garrick's version affects the design of Berlioz's symphony, notably in No. 6 which, as Berlioz admitted, is otherwise barely comprehensible (see Appendix 1b). Nevertheless Berlioz was firmly independent in other respects, owing surprisingly little to the specifics of the Kemble version. The opening quarrel, the ball, the *Scène d'amour* and the Queen Mab speech (only a little abbreviated by Garrick) are common to all versions; these are reflected in the most symphonic sections (*Introduction* in No. 1; No. 2; No. 3 after the chorus; No. 4). Garrick's tomb scene was retained by Kemble (No. 6), but Berlioz returned to Garrick for the *Convoi funèbre* (No. 5) which Kemble omitted, and went further back, to Shakespeare, to introduce two prologues (Garrick omitted both).

The finale is still further evidence of Berlioz's independence. He drew attention to the final scene in his preface (see Appendix 1a), even asserting that it had not been staged since Shakespeare's time. This claim would be hard to substantiate, given the existence of a truncated form of this scene in Garrick's version of the play, and Berlioz's version is hardly Shakespearean. Garrick continued beyond Juliet's death, with which Kemble concluded, but cut about eighty lines of retrospective explanation; he retained the arrival of the Prince to supervise an almost spontaneous reconciliation of the families. Thus it was Berlioz (one assumes, rather than Deschamps) who decided to make the final scene the largest movement, the culminating point of the whole experience, and to produce a grandly rhetorical argument for reconciliation from a representative of the Church rather than the state. Perhaps because Lawrence is a major character in the play, it was felt that, necessarily absent from the instrumental heart of the symphony, he deserved a role here; the Prince had appeared in the Prologue, represented by the brass choir whose voice enhances the closing stages of Lawrence's oration. Deschamps, perhaps influenced by Berlioz, retained Lawrence's oration in his version of the play. Whatever the authors' thinking, there is an undeniable change of emphasis: the reconciliation is at the hands of the Catholic Church, with an explicit reliance on the healing power of the Cross.[20]

Exordium: Introduction *and Prologue;* Roméo seul

After the *Symphonie fantastique* and *Harold en Italie* Berlioz might have been expected to bind the movements of his longest symphony together by another melodic *idée fixe*. But here there is no dramatic *idée fixe* to which music can stand as analogue. Instead Berlioz uses overt thematic anticipation (in the Prologue) and reminiscences in the later movements; in addition, consciously or otherwise, he included some less evident cross-references, a systematic account of which is beyond the scope of the present study.

No. 1 Introduction and Prologue

Combats – Tumulte –   Fighting – riot –
Intervention du Prince   intervention of the Prince

The 'Allegro fugato' ($\d = 116$) begins as a series of fugal entries. This is a favourite opening gambit of Berlioz; but where the beginnings of *Harold en Italie* and *La Damnation de Faust* are fugal meditations, this is fast and furious, vividly suggesting the stage filling with quarrelling citizens. The subject (Ex. 4.1A) is abrasive, characterized by crisp trills on the dotted notes, staccato (forte) articulation, and a sense of getting nowhere fast which results from its sinking at the end to the F♯ from which it originally sprang. The cello answer, tonally altered, is even more angular.[1]

The obvious associations of fugue are academic, regular: Berlioz, who makes many and varied uses of fugal texture throughout *Roméo*, plays on this expectation to create disorder. The violins enter in stretto and in 'wrong' keys; the firsts, in G, are leapfrogged by the seconds two bars later in B minor, then they grapple at one-bar intervals (bars 13, 14) in D and F♯ minor. This contributes to a frenetic crescendo assisted by the piecemeal entry of woodwinds from bar 14. The texture becomes fuller and less contrapuntal above the bass entry in F♯ minor (bar 19). At bar 24 the first brass appear, horns providing solidity to a tonic pedal: the rioting is gripped by its own momentum, reaching critical mass. The pedal lasts thirteen bars, with brilliant

Ex. 4.1A

Ex. 4.1B

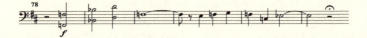

strettas whose insistence on the high g″ (flutes g‴) compels the shift to dominant harmony at bar 38. Then the music plunges into D major. The fresh key suggests an arrival, and the fugue subject is merrily combined with a new theme. In the play, the trouble begins with servants; the swagger and irresponsibility of upper-class youth, who arrive spoiling for a fight, is embodied in the jaunty trombone phrase (bar 44).[2] Berlioz also adds fourth horn and in due course timpani and cornets, leaving few orchestral resources untapped before a climactic rhythmic shock: at bar 54, the second violins and woodwind persevere with the fugue subject, still in D; the trombones rise in severely duple rhythm, heterophonically doubled in crotchet triplets by the string basses; and timpani, horns, flutes, and first violins accentuate apparent bars of $\frac{3}{4}$.

Massive cadences in D major (bars 60–5) invite interpretation in terms of a sonata-form exposition, but they turn back towards the local dominant, A (65–8). Berlioz may have intended an effect by creating, then contradicting, the idea of a sonata. Moreover, just as the intervention of the prince curbs the riot, so Berlioz curbs the timbral and textural excesses of its musical metaphor. A heavy diminished seventh breaks into the A major harmony, and the tonality ceases to cohere. Then there is a new direction, which inflects the main tempo: 'Fièrement, un peu retenu et avec le caractère du récitatif'.

Berlioz 'set' the Prince's intervention as instrumental recitative, one of few elements in the conception of *Roméo et Juliette* for which he was directly indebted to Beethoven's Ninth.[3] But while in both the tempo is fast, Berlioz's note-values are long, beginning with the fugue theme in massive augmentation

(Ex. 4.1B). This transformation of a theme to mean the opposite of its original presentation is a device related to the *idée fixe*; in the *Symphonie fantastique*, the melody in the first movement is a metaphor for the chaste and remote image of the beloved, whereas in the finale the image is both tawdry and depraved. However, in that instance both versions represented an image of the same person, whereas here the similarity is the situation, the riot which the first version of the theme foments and the second quells.[4]

The 'recitative', confided to heavy brass (ophicleide, three trombones, and horns as far as possible, given their mechanical limitations), is punctuated by the fugue-subject – a subdued muttering from the rioters – while the neighbour-note figure is taken up in a strange sequence by the 'Prince' (from bar 111). His anger is represented by tonal arbitrariness: there seems no way of predicting which key may be reinforced. Berlioz structures the passage by breaking from unison brass into full triadic harmony (bar 135); then ending the brass's rhythmic unison (from bar 147), as if the Prince is challenging the different families by turns (they respond with muttered string pizzicato); then by a searing dissonance (bar 155) just before the huge B major cadence. The dispersal of the combatants is graphically depicted by the liquidation of the fugue subject onto an eventual dominant pedal. The main bass note is the upper neighbour, G, with the trill from the subject; but there is no room for ambiguity in the resolution, and the close, with its growing silences, is stage-clearing music, a subdued reversal of the opening.

Prologue

The second part of No. 1 has neither a thematic nor a presentational connection with the first. The dominant chord (F♯ major) lingers, repeated by the harp, which Berlioz considered traditional for narration.[5] Berlioz's Prologue has two aims: to sing, in effect, the programme of the symphony, and to introduce some of its themes. The text is given in Appendix 2, in both the original and revised forms. Its account of the action might be considered cryptic if one did not know the play; it seems to have been Berlioz's assumption (challenged only partly by his inscription to No. 6: see Appendix 1b) that his audience had a grasp of the outline plot.

The problem of narration in a concert work has received many and various solutions, but Berlioz's 'Prologue en récitatif harmonique' has not been imitated. Yet performed with the right sense of commitment, it gives rise to moments of expressive beauty within a starkly simple idiom that lies outside the mainstream of nineteenth-century music. The chorus declaims mainly in unison (particularly in the rejected second Prologue) or in rhythmic unison, to a slow progression of simple triads. Harmony is expressive, therefore, by virtue of being the only musical element subject to variation. The sections below are numbered in accordance with the libretto (Appendix 2).

(1) The chorus explains what we have already heard. From a bald opening, in unison or in dyads on the main pitches of the prevailing tonality (B minor), a move towards D is articulated by triads (bars 11–16). The first orchestral intervention is a sombre D minor chord for brass and timpani, with crescendo and diminuendo, a timbral recall of the Prince's intervention and a hint of future tragedy.

(2) An expressive modulation (D to F♯ minor) introduces the 'plot' of the symphony's No. 2 (Romeo alone; Capulet's ball). Loneliness is symbolized by the entry of a solo contralto whose line meanders from F♯ to A, preparing, after further choral intervention, for the entry of the ball music. The definitive version of this passage (from bar 36) initiates the function of the Prologue as 'thematic catalogue'; it presents the ball music in its principal form on woodwind, in A major, and a $\frac{6}{8}$ transformation on strings in F major (bar 56), reversing the tonalities of this material in No. 2 (the ball itself, in F) and No. 3 (the young Capulets' chorus in A): the modulation, orchestral as well as tonal, is charmingly handled.[6]

(3) 'La fête est terminée' suggests a description of No. 3 (*Scène d'amour*) to follow. But Berlioz does not intend such literalism. Romeo's sighs (cellos, bar 69) are represented not by reference to the opening stages of No. 3, but by a motive from No. 2 *(Roméo seul)*, there in F, here in D major.[7] This tonality enables Berlioz to ascend two fifths, to E, at the next full orchestral entry, a quotation from the height of the love-scene (bar 91). In these extracts, the chorus abandons its austere recitative and joins in music which is not otherwise presented vocally.[8] The path from D to E is indirect, and may serve as an example of Berlioz's rhetorical method in this Prologue. A first gesture which could reach A emerges into C (the harmonic scheme is given in Ex. 4.2). The unison is filled out harmonically, the three-part chorus divided into five and underpinned by low-pitched strings, pianissimo: this is 'la blanche Juliette', already on her balcony. The harmony progresses diatonically (C–a–d) and then, a touch of magic, chromatically (d–C♯).[9] Diminished triads continue the ambiguity of the chord-succession, only to burst forth into the love-theme. Berlioz cadences this section rather perversely in E minor, his intention perhaps to prepare tonally for the next section, which is in G.

(4) The Prologue is interrupted by the 'Strophes', a song which Berlioz originally composed for voice and guitar, later preferring the orchestrally more conformable harp. We step outside the summary development of the plot to

Ex. 4.2

meditate on the beauty of the scene: not so much the moonlit night in the orchard as the beauty of innocent first love, for Romeo (we assume, following Garrick's version), has not loved before; Shakespeare is more earthy.

'Strophes' is found dull or ravishing by different listeners, or even by the same listener in different performances. This is not hard to understand, for it demands suspension of the wish for dramatic development. Moreover it is not a purely lyric meditation, despite its clearly lyric form of two strophes, but a continuation of the spirit of the recitative; Deschamps' poem is declaimed in a wonderfully controlled melodic arch whose individual building-blocks are too simple to strike the hearer as melodically significant. The effect, then, is the opposite of a typical Berlioz lyric, with its tendency to flower into a memorable and characteristic turn of phrase (as in, for instance, *La captive*). The calm development of the long musical paragraph and the monotony of the harp accompaniment (for all its gradual animation from semiquavers to triplets and demisemiquavers) are subtly varied by interpolations from high woodwind, including one of the symphony's most characteristic voices, the cor anglais.[10] At the cadence ('Dans le ciel') the prologue chorus enters and at the repeat a delicate cello obbligato enlivens the second verse, a detail appreciated by several critics in 1839.

These musical features, notably its reticence, are designed to distance 'Strophes' from the rest of the symphony. Berlioz stands back from his own creation and invites us, not to admire it, but to admire its source. We are no longer listening to an introductory narrative, but an alienation: the symphonic movements will be based, not on a story, but on Shakespeare's play. Thus Shakespeare alone possessed the secret of the 'premiers transports', and he has taken it with him to heaven. Nevertheless Berlioz intends us to penetrate these secrets, although the honeyed cup will be withdrawn by the jealous angels: Romeo and Juliet are punished, one might infer, for their temerity in feeling such perfect mutual love. It is not an interpretation of Shakespeare which sits well with the jingle and quibble, with which Berlioz had no more truck than Garrick.

(5) The tenor solo here is not Mercutio but another narrative voice.[11] The Queen Mab speech appeared in the play before Romeo and Juliet had met. Berlioz has Mercutio poke fun at Romeo after the love-scene, as in Shakespeare's II.4; this may explain the order of the symphonic movements, which from a musical point of view needs no apology. This brilliant Scherzetto sets a version of the speech which later forms the basis of No. 4. Doubtless to avoid redundancy Berlioz makes only the most generalized musical links between the two movements: a contrast of high and low instrumentation (here piccolo, flute, violas, cellos and basses), light articulation (including *pizzicato*), F major as a key, and a conventional quasi-glissando cadence. The magical atmosphere is thus close to the Scherzo, but the motives and rhythms (including the duple metre) are distinct; although similar modulations are used, they are harmonic shifts one might expect in any Berlioz piece in F major.[12]

(6) After this delicacy, Berlioz originally closed his prologue with an apologia derived from the last two lines of Shakespeare's prologue, but intended to justify the use of orchestral music for the central scenes (see Appendix 2). The rest of the plot was outlined in the second Prologue. On abandoning the latter, Berlioz revised the end of No. 1 but included only generalized sentiments preparing for the tragic outcome, together with a last thematic anticipation, the chiming bells and fugue theme of No. 5 (*Convoi funèbre*); no guidance is offered to the listener for No. 6 (*Roméo au tombeau des Capulets*), nor is there any preparation for the Finale. The Prologue links to No. 2 tonally; a deep sigh on an A minor triad for full orchestra responds to the D minor chord near the opening.[13]

No. 2

Roméo seul – Tristesse – Concert et Bal.[14] Grande Fête chez Capulet.	Romeo alone: sadness – Concert and Ball. Great festivity at Capulet's.

According to the symphonic conception of *Roméo et Juliette*, this is the 'first movement', a slow introduction and Allegro. This interpretation is thwarted as much by the form of the music as by the programmatic elements which give rise to it. There are two slow sections, neither introductory in character, and the Allegro is decidedly unlike even the semblance of sonata form used by Berlioz in the *Symphonie fantastique* and *Harold en Italie*, and still less like the relatively clear forms of his overtures.[15] This is not to suggest that a symphonic Allegro has to be in sonata form; only that every precedent and contemporary comparison suggests it.

Ex. 4.3

(1) *Andante malinconico e sostenuto* ($\downarrow$ = 66)

The gradual focusing and intensification of this passage suggests that Romeo's thoughts become increasingly fixed upon a single passion (love) which develops a particular object. Berlioz's treatment conveys the erotic nature of the attraction, but a sense of awe governs the mysterious opening, as well as the loneliness reminiscent of the 'mal d'isolement' of the *Symphonie fantastique*.[16] A melody in the violins marked *ppp* winds down the chromatic scale from high F (Ex. 4.3) while proposing as motives a rising fourth (x), a dotted rhythm (y), and a segment of the chromatic scale articulated in various ways (z + number of steps). Perhaps the least unusual aspect of this theme is its length and harmonic outline: it is a four-bar phrase, the rising fourth proposes the tonality of F, and the return to C is enhanced by a gentle confirmatory pizzicato. The second phrase, however, takes the premises of the first to an unexpected conclusion. The descending chromatic line continues, to B; (x) is now a sixth, (y) is reduplicated, and the top C is resolved back to the octave of the initial B. The rising fourth of the first phrase was answered by a chromatic return to the original pitch, but the second closes with a quasi dominant-to-tonic fall of a perfect fifth. Berlioz colours this remote modulation (to E major or minor, but conceived more colouristically than organically) by the first wind entry.

Chromatic sleight of hand leads to a reprise (phrase 3) and further variations of the uncertainly brooding violin line. But confidence grows when phrase 3 mirrors phrase 1 but leaps up, ending on F; phrase 4 (bar 14) eliminates the

Ex. 4.4

nervy dotted rhythm (y). The symbolic loneliness of the violins is gradually eroded: the lower strings join the A minor cadence at bar 16 and the wind figure in bar 17 ascends to prepare the f″ of their last phrase. The longest chromatic slide down arches reassuringly (bar 20) to a cadence in F major with a new textural continuum, violin semiquavers and viola tremolo.

The programmatic clue in Berlioz's movement-heading seems to equate the second section (from bar 22) with 'Tristesse', but there is no need to subdivide the movement so literally. As it assimilates the opening directionlessness into tonal and textural continuity, the passage suggests sadness rather less than the opening. Romeo's lonely meditation is now focused. This marvellous section raises one textural and programmatic question: although it represents the feelings of Romeo, the melody is predominantly in a high register. But the explanation may be simply that it represents Romeo thinking: when he utters, in the *Scène d'amour* and the invocation, he becomes an instrumental tenor. We have heard this melody in the Prologue, at 'Hélas, Roméo soupire', there referring to the time after the ball. Before that encounter with Juliet, the same melody's repeated surges, its repetitions accumulating instrumental power (two winds, three winds, four winds and violins), and its gentle release suggest a tender eroticism. The third repetition of the four-note motive drains its energy back to the dominant (reversing the movement of bar 1) only to surge anew to c‴, then higher (Ex. 4.4). A powerful diminished seventh on B♮ seems to point inexorably to a tonic cadence, but the bass slides down to E♭ and the cadence is in A♭. This sort of altered mediant especially attracted Berlioz and has its own value as colour, but the preceding tonic minor elements allow it a degree of naturalness.

A delicate strain on solo wind undulates towards C major where Berlioz completes a thematic ternary design by a reprise of the sighing melody, intensified by its higher pitch. But Berlioz is not yet ready to expose the dominant key fully (it would indeed be unusual in a slow introduction).[17] The melody thrusts to f″ and dies back; the cadence-formula (bars 55–6) is repeated in the flutes and its final phrase in the low strings. This cadence too is interrupted, and the inception of the Allegro anticipated, by a brief intimation of the motive of the ball. We have heard this tune in the Prologue, so we know what it represents; a whisper of it appeared as early as bars 8–9 (see Ex. 4.3). But here it is only a fragment blown on the wind, sinking into themeless tremolo and then only heard (how like a modern dance) as a throbbing of percussion.

(2) *Larghetto espressivo* ($\downarrow = 58$)

The melody (Ex. 4.5) unfolds as a long Berliozian paragraph. A short first phrase (five bars, 82–6) closes on its point of initiation, the mediant E, and is followed by a much longer extension (bars 87–107), although this subdivides after another five bars. This point, bar 91, appears to be a reprise of the opening (but the harmony is A minor, not C). The irregular sequential growth of the end of the melody is especially characteristic, as is the choice of oboe as 'singer' or representative of Juliet. Apart from the insistent recurrence of the rhythm of the ball which adds to the fragility of the image, the passage is characterized by purity; the harmony, unlike that of 'Roméo seul', is diatonic

Ex. 4.5

with only touches of chromaticism which grow towards the end – the near-chromatic slide from the top e''' (bars 98–100) and the flattened sixth degree descending by leap (104–5), a reference to the leap of a sixth down to the tonic which characterized the end of the opening theme (bar 36). Nevertheless, Ex. 4.5 shows the close involvement of motives from Ex. 4.3 and confirms this melody as an integral part of Romeo's meditation.

Berlioz's original heading could be read as meaning that the distant sound of the ball is followed by a (distant) 'concert'; bar 22 would then represent 'tristesse' and the oboe solo, whose harp-imitation accompaniment (reminiscent of 'Strophes') undoubtedly suggests formal song, becomes the 'concert'.[18] This concert has no place in Shakespeare or any subsequent version of the play, however, nor does Berlioz allude to it in the Prologue. In any case, the Larghetto, whose melody returns with such power during the following Allegro, cannot be trivialized into a mere interlude. For Ernest Newman this, 'one of the most moving melodies ever entrusted to a solo oboe', was clearly a 'Romeo melody'.[19] It surely also represents an image of Juliet, upon whom Romeo's erotic fascination is now fixed: the song is a metaphor for Juliet's image. This is surely the only programmatic, as distinct from formal, explanation for its *forte* recurrence during the ball, its dominance as a fragment thereafter, and its gentle echo at the end of the movement, not to mention the broken reminiscence of it which ends *Roméo au tombeau* (No. 6; see Chapter 6).

30

(3) *Allegro* ($\downharpoonright = 108$)

The rhythmic accompaniment pulses throughout the oboe melody, notated in small values to approximate to the fast tempo. Berlioz begins the Allegro proper with this rhythm (violins) while building a crescendo on another intimation of the main theme (Ex. 4.6B) in the basses; this is a diatonic version which surges to the harmonic danger-point of a major ninth in fourth inversion (bar 113).[20] The main characteristics of this theme are its descending motion and the phrasing in paired quavers. At bar 115 Berlioz breaks into staccato (strings then wind) and a brief uproar with notably fine harmony precedes a dominant climax and fermata. Thus harmonically the whole passage reinterprets C, the tonic of Ex. 4.5, as a dominant of F; and the remainder of the movement barely leaves this key.

The Allegro at first follows a rondo-like pattern.[21]

Bar 129. Full exposure of the main theme (Ex. 4.6A; note the persistence of 'z'), tutti (except trombones), including chromatic extension of the cadence period (the flat sixth, d♭''', bar 152).

Bar 156, episode. The paired quaver is replaced by chattering woodwind over a figure (a male dancer?) in the bass instruments which brusquely contradicts the tonality by entering on E♭, only to resolve it as Neapolitan to D minor. Sequence down a tone (D♭) brings the dominant (166) and a nonchalant move to the tonic (171), ingratiatingly syncopated. This is followed by a Rossini-like figure using triplets; the texture is capriciously disintegrated before settling onto a long trill and turns into:

Bar 187. Abbreviated reprise, lightly scored with harp-like accompaniment and a silvery winding violin counterpoint.

Bar 206. Second episode, foreshadowing the return of 'Romeo's song'. We may infer that Romeo has caught a glimpse of Juliet through the milling bodies. The opening of Ex. 4.5 is counterpointed with new dance material, flung easily from wind to strings and back like an alternation of sexes in dance movements; this idea becomes important in the last stages of the movement. The tonality is briefly disrupted, again with minor-mode elements on the flat side of F. A♭ resolves to G for another broken-textured passage of irresistible charm, 215–19.[22] A conflict of G and D♭ brings back the rumbustious spirit; but with further insouciance Berlioz trips a fragment of the melody back to F.

Bar 225 (upbeat). Second reprise. Berlioz heads this section (at bar 226) 'Réunion des deux Thèmes, du Larghetto et de l'Allegro', the former (Ex. 4.5) unfolding in vast 'bars' of three semibreves. This procedure is

Ex. 4.6A

Ex. 4.6B

Ex. 4.6C

Ex. 4.6D

rhetorically similar to the 'Ronde du Sabbat' (*Symphonie fantastique*) and the overture *Benvenuto Cellini*. But in those two very different movements the 'reunion' forms part of the last climactic peroration; this one comes at about the mid-point of the movement.[23] 'Romeo's song' sings out in the wind, except the trumpets which cannot play it and the first flute which doubles the ball theme. The section thus functions as a second reprise of the 'rondo' and a reprise, and tonal resolution, of the song-theme, previously exposed in the dominant.[24] The effect, however, is monolithic rather than contrapuntal; the purity of the song-theme allows it to combine with the harmonically static surface activity of the ball over an almost continuous tonic pedal. The ball theme eventually has to develop new extensions to fit with the slow melody, which thus dominates the proceedings as if Romeo were singing his heart out to Juliet.

Bar 266. Episode 3. The reunion ends with another deceptive resolution (a sudden A major harmony). The duplet quavers of the ball theme characterize music which is otherwise broken in texture as it slows over a tremolo. The movement is reanimated by a programmatic conception which Berlioz finally omitted from his explanatory Prologue. The threats of Tybalt are represented by an ostensibly new chromatic figure which, however, may also be regarded as a distorted version of the main dance theme. It emerges in the bassoons (Ex. 4.6C) following a violin diminuendo, and reaches a definitive form as a four-bar basso ostinato from bars 286–9.[25] In addition the main ball theme is transformed in a brief fugato introduced by the bassoons in bar 278 and accumulating threateningly until 293: it will be recalled that an abrasive fugato has already represented rioting in No. 1.

Bar 294. Peroration. Tybalt is quelled by old Capulet, and the dance mood is restored with the arrival on a comparatively undisturbed dominant, represented by a high violin tremolo. This is only a lightly articulated division, as the ostinato has already established a four-bar momentum; but at bar 294 it settles into the dominant position, nine full statements underpinning a massive crescendo to bar 329. The higher registers at first seem uncertain, repeating the main percussion rhythm (echoed by horns) until the peak at bar 318; here material from the second episode is again tossed about. The ostinato ends with a held dominant which the next passage prolongs by a variety of local harmonic gestures: the material alternates ascending string scales with wind flutters. In a ballet, these might denote aggressive males, coquettish females: certainly the atmosphere is heated and suggests social indiscretion, confirmed by the young Capulets at the opening of No. 3. The first manoeuvre is to D minor (bar 235), quitted by a circle of fifths (G–C–F). As in a game of courtship the moves are repeated (348 = 332) and the C stage extended (360) to reach an unarticulated tonic at bar 367, followed by a tutti (at last!) and decisive cadence at 374–5.

Coda 375–414. The coda, in formal terms a résumé of material, begins with a series of exuberant cadences based on the main ball theme, practically unheard since the threat from Tybalt. His ostinato enters on E♭, and the subdominant implication is elegantly composed out by counterpointing it with the song-theme, restored to the oboe above the rhythm of the dance (timpani): a farewell which distances us, with our Romeo-perspective, from the scene of the festivities and its lodestar, Juliet. The main tempo is restored for a final blaze of glory, though the Tybalt-ostinato is revived nearly at the end.[26]

5

The heart of the matter: Scène d'amour; La reine Mab

No. 3 Scène d'amour

Nuit sereine – Le Jardin de Capulet
silencieux et désert.
Les jeunes Capulets sortant de la fête,
passent en chantant des réminiscences
de la musique de bal.

Peaceful night – Capulet's garden,
silent and deserted.
Young Capulets leaving the party
pass by singing remembered
phrases of the dance music.

Allegretto ($\downarrow$. = 92)

[Double chorus of male Capulets]
Ohé, Capulets, bonsoir, bonsoir!
Ohé, bonsoir, cavaliers au revoir!
Ah, quelle nuit, quel festin!
Bal divin, quel festin . . .
Que de folles paroles . . .
Belles Véronaises
Sous les grand mélêzes,
Allez rêver de bal et d'amour
 Jusqu'au jour.
Tra la la la!
La belle fête . . .
Dames Véronaises . . .
Allez rêver de bal et d'amour.

Yo, Capulets, good night!
Yo, goodnight, boys, ciao for now!
Ah, what a night, what a ball!
What a fabulous dance.
What crazy talk . . .
Lovely girls of Verona
Underneath those high larch-trees,
Go dream of dancing and love
 Till dawn comes.
Tra la la la!
What a great party . . .
Dames of Verona . . .
Go dream of dancing and love.

Adagio

Juliette sur son balcon et Roméo dans
l'ombre. Scène d'amour.
Orchestre seul.

Juliet on her balcony and Romeo
in the shadow. Love-scene.
Orchestra alone.[1]

The *Scène d'amour* from *Roméo et Juliette* is 'the movement which three-quarters of the musicians of Europe that know it rate above everything I have written'.[2] Many critics have agreed with Berlioz, one calling it 'the finest piece

35

of music that ever came out of Gaul'.[3] Its outstanding quality does not, however, make for easy analysis: rather the contrary. The movement falls into no traditional form; and while it is clearly programmatic, its relation to the balcony scene which inspired it is hardly clearer than the combined dramatic motifs which make up No. 2. The Prologue reminds us that Romeo leaps the garden wall; in the play he conceals himself from his friends as well as from the Capulets, who would kill him if they found him. To make it clear whose territory we are on, Berlioz and Deschamps devised a short chorus, based on a simplistic version of the main dance tune of No. 2 (see above, Ex. 4.6D) and thus the first instance of thematic cross-reference between the principal movements.

Before the chorus Berlioz offers a musical analogue for the shadowy silence of the orchard. Marked Allegretto to conform to the Capulets' song, the opening is deceptive in metre and tempo; the first 34 bars have no internal subdivision and the note-lengths, usually of two bars, fall into no consistent phraseology. Only a three-note melodic curve ('x' in Ex. 5.1) provides a recurring pattern. The harmony is still more disorientating, or at least the true tonality is defined only gradually. In five bars Berlioz has reached the opposite tonal pole, E♭, in the unstable, and unresolved, second inversion (see Ex. 5.1). In the background, the high register couples the dominant pitch e' to e", but by way of an E♭ (or D♯) arpeggio; at the high point (bar 35) the swaying horn figure, a first binary division of the $\frac{6}{8}$ bar, helps establish the dominant harmony which broadly prevails until the revellers launch into their serenade-like reminiscence at bar 49. Ex. 5.1 is an outline, designed to show the limited periodicity of the violin part and the gradual stabilization of the harmony.

Ex. 5.1

This double chorus of Capulets is in ternary form, the outer sections based on the main ball theme, the middle (the 'Tra la la') on a later episode (No. 2, from bar 207 and 318). Its charm is enhanced by being sung, in the interests of realism, off stage. This allows some of the listener's attention to focus on a tentative development within the orchestra; an ascending scale underlines the chorus, rising over two octaves in the cellos; it reappears as a four-note unit in cellos and violas under the middle section of the chorus, guiding the tipsy modulations.[4] The sustained string sound is gradually increased to three or four parts as the chorus proceeds, then reduced to the divided cellos and separate double-basses to establish the texture of the Adagio. Berlioz interrupts the Capulets' cadence with an ironic emphasis from the double-basses who descend to G♮ (108) where A is expected; they resolve it upwards, a manoeuvre which recurs later in this movement and in No. 6.[5] The strings cease, leaving the distant voices on a gently glowing six-part tonic triad.

The Adagio

Here Berlioz curbed his affection for contrast by retaining A major harmony and the $\frac{6}{8}$ metre. Even the pulse is scarcely changed, with the Adagio ♪ = 88 only a little slower than the ♩. = 92 of the Allegretto. Throughout the movement Berlioz directs subtle changes of this quaver pulse by tempo directions and metronomic indications; most of it should go more quickly than the opening. These directions require a fluctuation of tempo corresponding to the flux of passions ('vague des passions') experienced by the lovers.[6] In contrast to the rhythmless opening and the three-directional chorus, however, is the homogeneous choir of low strings with intricate subdivisions of the bar. The bird-like motive in the second violins ('x' in Ex. 5.2A) is superimposed to provide a further element in the polyphony, while rich chromatic inflections and occasional modulation seldom threaten tonal orientation.

Above this rich *pianissimo* tapestry, to which sustained horns or bassoons are added, a tentative song emerges on the octave coupling of clarinet and cor anglais (Ex. 5.2B).This is at first recognizable as an expansion of 'x'. Its slow melodic growth, closing the silences by accumulation in pitch and rhythm, is punctuated by delicate rising shapes, including an equally bird-like trill, from the first violins. The brief, intense climax turns towards the mediant, C♯ minor, a modulation beautifully overturned by the second paragraph of the Adagio.

Programmatically this is fairly transparent. The balcony scene begins with Juliet's soliloquy; Romeo responds from the shadows. Juliet is represented by

Ex. 5.2A

Ex. 5.2B

Ex. 5.2C

the high woodwind, Romeo by cellos and horns. Juliet turns wistfully to the minor mediant; Romeo glowingly returns to the tonic. Programmatically, however, the opening dialogue cannot be precisely correlated with the play. The scene begins with a monologue for Romeo; here Juliet speaks first (if we have any doubt that the high woodwind represent her it is dispelled by the reprise of this material at the moment of her awakening in No. 6). After Romeo's response, the whole exchange is repeated: Juliet's second strophe (from bar 155), compressed, more intense in texture, but not modulating, Romeo's reply, now a glowing fortissimo (172), in the altered mediant, C major.[7] It is tempting to understand Romeo's first speech as inaudible, preparation for the declaration in the second which Juliet hears and to which she responds in the next (Allegro agitato) section. But such doubtful literalism is needed only to support a parallel (of which Berlioz gave no hint) between the sequence of speeches in the balcony scene and the development of the music. In reality the music cannot be reconciled to the naturalistic movement of Shakespeare's dialogue. It is better understood as a tonally open but satisfying musical period conveying the essence of an emotional exchange in musical terms.

The Allegro agitato ($\textstyle\quad$ = 152) develops figure 'x' (Ex. 5.2C) almost exclusively, Juliet's 'voice' now an intriguing doubling of flute and oboe.[8] Romeo's response in the cellos takes the form of recitative. This section may reflect Juliet's startled response at finding herself addressed with words of love from the darkness ('I take thee at thy word. Call me but love, and I'll be new baptiz'd . . .'; to which she replies 'What man art thou, that, thus bescreen'd in night, So stumblest on my counsel?'). Similarly we may associate the longest speech in the scene (Juliet: 'Thou knows't the mask of night is on my face . . .') with the extended solo for flute and cor anglais in F# minor at the return to Adagio (bar 243, the melody starting in earnest at 250). But we may also relish this development for its own beauty, and as a musical contrast. What is certain is that the later development of the music as we know it parallels the balcony scene only in its broadest outlines; for if Berlioz originally adhered to a programme, he effectively discarded it when revising the movement. The autograph retains signs of two cuts of unknown length. The first implies a development of the F# minor melody, now in A minor (which might call into question its association with that particular speech); it is not replaced by any equivalent. If the movement was originally programmatic in detail, therefore, it no longer is, and Berlioz clearly regarded musical proportion as of greater importance in making his revision.[9]

This is not to say that the music is not programmatic, nor even that Berlioz ignored dramatic development in favour of musical form; few of his movements are so remote from traditional archetypes, and the search for a musical framework within which to understand the argument is likely to be fruitless unless we consider the 'real' programme: the musical exploration of the 'premiers transports' of the prologue's 'Strophes'. The general direction of the movement corresponds to the balcony scene. It proceeds from distinct voices in dialogue (the first Adagio; the Allegro; the long melody opening the second Adagio) which are musical equivalents to declaration, agitation, reassurance (the cello recitative) and the exploration of the situation (the second Adagio). It then suggests that the intricate feelings of the participants are merged in surges of passion, threatened by an intrusion (bar 334, see below), and ending in a lingering farewell. This is surely programme enough.

The second Adagio (bar 243, rather faster at ♪ = 112) expands over a new accompaniment. Rather than the pictorial background of the first Adagio (Ex. 5.2A), this is a gentle pulsation with an independent double-bass line – whether representing a submerged threat or the barely suppressed excitement of the lovers it is impossible to say. Juliet's 'speech' takes the cor anglais from her first utterance (bar 127) and the flute from her second (the Allegro), to build a melodic arch: its hesitant opening in the minor key (bar 248) takes flight from bar 250 in a lyrical questing which restores the tonic A major but repeatedly postpones a secure cadence (until bar 274 where a new section begins). Berlioz's tactic of elliptical closure of a section into the opening of the next contributes a seamless quality of growth matched on the surface by the general continuity of tonality (A major is never absent for more than a few bars) and the continual development of motives and their accompaniments which replaces discrete sections of development and recapitulation.

From bar 274 the structure is secured by the return of a new, yet composite, melody (Ex. 5.3), based on both 'Juliet' and 'Romeo' material. This functions as a rondo-like refrain over the last 110 bars; its relative stability, however, is qualified by continual transformations of the idea and its setting, while the inexact, organic development of what would be rondo episodes (as in the ball scene) defeats explanation in such classical terms.[10]

The refrain, with Juliet's 'x' figure expanded and Romeo's cadence, is at a slightly slower tempo, and at first the melody is in the high (Juliet) register. If the theme represents their spiritual union, therefore, it suggests that (as in Shakespeare) Juliet is the leader of the scene, the less poetically impassioned and more practical. The refrains come in pairs; a recitative in Romeo's register (violas and cellos) leads to a repeat (bar 286) with the melody doubled by violins and cellos as if the two voices are finally joined. Even here there is variation, however, for the descending semi-chromatic line of the woodwind now starts a third lower, from c♯''' not e''', and the accompaniment is adapted from that of the F♯ minor theme (compare bars 286 and 251).

Ex. 5.3

This cadence is barely reached at bar 292 when an episode is launched. The music is layered; a winding woodwind theme is developed against insecure syncopations in the strings and horns which prove the more significant factor later as, perhaps, does the sighing alternation of wind and strings from bar 300.[11] The episode moves to the dominant (bars 304–8, the triplets reminiscent of the *Scène aux champs*), but its cadence is again overwhelmed by the syncopated idea which drives passionately through an ambiguous harmonic sequence to the tonic minor at bar 317. A descending line, augmented at its third statement, acts as transition to a slower tempo and the return of the refrain at bar 322, very much as at first; the interlude between two statements develops this violin line, further enhancing the sense of continuity of musical thought, even in a section where Berlioz cut an episode.

The repeat of the refrain is given by clarinets in thirds, a new texture which again recalls an operatic duet. Here, however, the outside world threatens with jolting violin figures (bars 333 and 334) and a sweeping scale (bar 336). Doubtless this represents the off-stage voice of Juliet's nurse, a grating intrusion of the mundane into Shakespeare's poetic lyricism which, in the symphony, might be criticized as inappropriately literary.[12] But it is the mundane, as in *Tristan*, which will overcome the lovers; and the first two violent phrases embody a traditional motive of death.[13] The scalar extension in bar 336 rises to a dissonant f♮‴ but is resolved in a sweet descant to the cadence of the love-theme (above the G–G♯–A motive). The high register thus attained is reconciled by the following descent; and the scale reappears as the generator of highest passion a few bars later.

The final phase of the movement is transformed by this rough interjection. The texture reduces to dialogue (bar 340), the cellos questioning, the violins' reply developing an intensification of motives from the love theme over a syncopated bass. The farewell is prolonged and difficult. A bar's silence leads to the last phrase of the refrain, its cadence again refused, and chromatic transformations of the motive lead the music to new harmonic regions, ultimately the dominant of E♭ (bar 355). This remote key is again evaded (compare Ex. 5.1) as the lovers return for a final exchange. The tempo animates (Ex. 5.4), the development of the first part of the refrain implying a $\frac{9}{8}$ metre; the intrusive scales lead to the fullest articulation of the dominant key with the final climactic statement of Romeo's declaration, as in the prologue, in E major (from bar 368).[14] This highest ecstasy breaks at bar 372 into frantic dialogue (high syncopes for Juliet from the Allegro; one cello phrase of recitative) before a reluctant unwinding, the love-theme cadence uniting clarinets and violins, but broken by silences. The lingering footsteps

Ex. 5.4

of Romeo at the end are both musically expressive and programmatically precise.

Thus ends the most ambiguous of Berlioz's musical forms, analogue of the fearful, 'chaste delirium' of first love. No further emphasis – neither wedding nor second love-scene – is needed for their feelings to resonate through the remainder of the symphony as the memory of bliss so nearly attained, so easily destroyed.

| No. 4 La reine Mab, ou la fée des songes (Scherzo) | Queen Mab, or the dream fairy (Scherzo) |

Prestissimo, $\frac{9}{8}$ ($\downdownarrows$. = 138)

Contrast was certainly a consideration at this juncture. By removing Mercutio's speech until this point, and 'setting' it in the key of No. 2, Berlioz closes off the love-scene from its surroundings; the ball hopelessly terrestrial, the scherzo reflecting the charms and dangers of the unconscious. The opening is still more indeterminate than that of No. 3, a diminished seventh which resolves by a simple cycle of fifths from the dominant of G to F. This indeterminacy is not only harmonic. As in No. 3 (Ex. 5.1), there are no notes shorter than the whole bar; the first bar is a pause, with another in bar 4. Moreover the orchestration gives notice of quicksilver changeability, shifting between a small wind group and muted string groupings playing normally, pizzicato, and with 'saltato' bow-strokes.[15] Crisp trills (bar 10) conclude the introduction, but Berlioz planned a series of false starts, the main theme dying onto an alien c♯ (bar 27), followed by more ethereal, harmonically elusive pauses; a second attempt similarly dies on b♮ (bar 55). At bar 70 Berlioz provides a complete cadenced period of 24 bars. The first eight bars consist of 'till ready' bobbing by the middle strings; not before time, the melody takes a definite shape, cadencing in the dominant, and the period is exactly repeated.

This is the most stable passage in a kaleidoscopic movement; again, its form eludes easy classification. The first part (to bar 341) is patterned normally for a scherzo, through repeated sections (though after bar 94 they are written out). The music consists almost entirely of four-bar units, so that Liszt suggested it should be conducted with four-beat ($\frac{12}{8}$) bars.[16] A second half balancing the repeated bars 70–93 extends to bar 125, cadencing in the tonic. A new section explores the flat side of the key (F minor, A♭, D♭) but ends on the dominant (bar 134–7); it is repeated (to 153) with a countermelody in the woodwind. The next section picks this up in the major but mainly develops the principal theme through pointed modulations as far as B minor; Berlioz wittily diverts us back to F. He could have ended there but instead recapitulates the main theme; note the rhythmic ambiguity whereby the harmony arrives on the dominant at bar 181 five, rather than four, bars before the downbeat of the recapitulation (186). The flat-side section is placed a fourth higher (as is usual with subsidiary material in recapitulations) and the original pitches are restored from bar 258, including the move to B minor; Berlioz comically raises the resolution a tone (bar 289) to reach G major, but progression down by fifths quickly restores F for a further reprise initiated by bassoons (bar 310) and a spiky cadence. From bar 341 the mediant pitch A is established to prepare for the trio section.

The formal archetype of Scherzo and Trio at least is clear: the movement falls into three main sections (A, B, A'), but this archetype is only a background, for the opening A section is developed, not repeated, in A'. Bars 354–417 form, generically, a slow 'trio'; the music goes three times more slowly by virtue of being in $\frac{3}{4}$, each beat corresponding to a whole bar of $\frac{3}{8}$.[17] Material from the scherzo can thus be accommodated as an intrusion on the slow tempo. Before and after the trio the sections balance almost exactly: 353 bars of $\frac{3}{8}$ before and 352 after. The trio itself lasts the equivalent of 192 $\frac{3}{8}$ bars, but there is nothing unusual about its relative brevity. What arouses controversy is the unconventional reprise (A'), and the degree to which it is programmatic. Although such unorthodox features as the indeterminate opening and elaborate development of the reprise invite programmatic explanation, critics generally hostile to the composer have praised the movement for being 'pure'.[18] But whereas in the Prologue the lyrical section relating to the love-scene ('Strophes') is essentially a meditation outside the framework of the drama, the tenor solo ('Scherzetto') gives us, in detail, the programme of the scherzo.

This text (see Appendix 2) is divided into four stages. The first, 'Mab, la messagère fluette et légère', describes Mab and her nocturnal habits; it must correspond to the scherzo's A section. For all its mercurial temperament the music has a single governing topic, and no more complex interpretation seems warrantable. The second phase of the speech is a specific adventure ('dans le cerveau d'un page, qui rêve espiègle tour ou molle sérénade . . .') and corresponds to the D minor 'trio' whose melancholy tune, highly expressive modulatory scheme, and twangling accompaniment (pizzicato cellos and harps), constitute a serenade, qualified only by the buzzing of Mab herself when the violas recall the main theme.[19]

This much is hardly controversial. But the scherzo reprise (A') has to accommodate two more adventures, each of which has roughly the same duration as the Trio.[20] Berlioz begins as if planning an orthodox reprise: a short transition returns to F and the main theme enters on cue at bar 430. But it is developed fugally, though with a full texture.[21] The third entry is extended sequentially and a full cadence is reached, so that the period from 431 to 474 is closed; it represents a return, therefore, to Mab herself, 'poursuivant sa promenade'. Resumption of a straightforward reprise is implied but repressed (at a point where Berlioz made a cut of unknown length);[22] the regular four-bar units are disrupted when the horn fanfare begins as if syncopated at bar 476 (Ex. 5.5).

Mab has landed 'sur le col bronzé d'un soldat'; he dreams of guns and trumpets . . . and wakes up cursing, to pray, then sleep and snore again. Horns normally evoke hunting rather than warfare,[23] but here they correspond to the soldier's dream, their wild modulations enabled by hand-horns in four different keys; the cannonade appears in the sinister crescendo of timpani and bass drum (from bar 556). The section is punctuated by the main theme, moving through various keys including A♭ major. Generically this is a

Ex. 5.5

44

development; the top of the crescendo (bar 583, after a shuddering duplet from the bass drum) is in D♭ major, with the main theme in the bassoons. The horn fanfares whimper, growing more distant and harmonically insecure over the throbbing of the timpani; D major bursts in from nowhere (bar 603).

Mab's final visit is to a girl – by analogy, Juliet – who dreams of a ball.[24] Before this destination becomes clear, Berlioz (from bar 609) threatens the momentum of her ride; the tremolo violas contain a hint of continuing violence, and the pauses remind us of the introduction to the movement, though here there is no diminished seventh. Berlioz further threatens the scherzo–trio model by making this an independent episode, melodically distinct but too short and structurally insecure to constitute a second Trio.[25] In a moment of magic the high harps begin a disembodied but glittering texture, enhanced by the two 'antique cymbals', as the background for a lightly leaping melody in the woodwind taken from *Le Ballet des ombres*.[26] Whether or not Berlioz had Juliet in mind in 1829 when he published and withdrew his original Opus 2, it is clearly apposite here; a dance of shades is generically similar, and musically indistinguishable, from revisiting a ball in a dream under Mab's influence. The issue is complicated by the rude entry of the bassoon on its lowest note (bar 631), *forte* against the prevailing *piano* background (the wind solos are *mezzo forte*): this is too clear an imitation of snoring not to be associated with the sleeping soldier. Far from being inattentive to his programme, however, Berlioz is imaginatively superimposing an element from one adventure onto the next to produce a grotesque Fuselian dream image – and at the same time effecting a characteristic structural economy. There remains only a brief reprise, from bar 661, of Mab's flight, with a diminuendo and ambiguous rallentando which refers to the introduction. A final flick of the antique cymbals and harps and an electric coda end this scintillating masterpiece.

La reine Mab stands aside from the other movements of *Roméo et Juliette* not because it is in any way 'abstract' but because, despite being placed at the centre of the symphony, it contains no cross-references to other movements; nor do voices refer it directly to the 'plot'. And, as has often been noted, it is misplaced in relation to the events of the play: Barraud says that it 'dramatiquement, n'a absolument rien à faire à ce moment de l'histoire'.[27] What, then, determined Berlioz to make it the centrepiece of his seven-movement conception?

The scherzo represents Mercutio, and thus a whole strand of the play. It is misplaced only in relation to his most famous speech; his role continues until he dies after the 'ball' and 'love-scene' at the hands of Tybalt (when Romeo declines to fight his wife's cousin: Act III scene 1). In its grotesque, irrational, and violent passages, which occur mainly in the reprise, the scherzo supplies the link between scenes of love (to which indeed it adds with its own Trio) and scenes of mourning. Ostensibly it is fairy music, yet this is not *A Mid-summer Night's Dream*; 'real' fairies have no place in naturalistic tragedy. But the deaths of Romeo and Juliet are brought about by irresponsibility, irrationality, midsummer madness; and by the rapier wit of Mercutio, which survives his wound ('ask for me tomorrow, and you will find me a grave man. I am peppered, I warrant, for this world. A plague o'both your houses!'), but which has prevented Romeo from proceeding with his speeches of conciliation and – who knows? – perhaps disarming the wrath of Tybalt.[28] The Mediterranean heat which makes young men boil into violence is indirectly represented by its nocturnal counterpart, the amoral dream-fairy whose elfin charm is the mask for bawdry and ugly practical jokes:

> This is that very Mab
> That plats the manes of horses in the night;
> And bakes the elf-locks in foul sluttish hairs,
> Which once untangled much misfortune bodes . . .

6

Tragedy and reconciliation: Convoi funèbre; Roméo au tombeau; *Finale*

No. 5 Convoi funèbre de Juliette

Marche fuguée INSTRUMENTALE d'abord, avec une psalmodie sur une seule note dans les voix: VOCALE ensuite, avec la psalmodie dans l'orchestre.

Fugal march, at first instrumental, with psalmody on a single note in the voices; then vocal, with the psalmody in the orchestra.

Andante non troppo lento ($\int$ = 72)

Choeur des Capulets:

Chorus of Capulets (mixed voices):

Jetez des fleurs pour la vierge expirée!
Jusqu'au tombeau, jetez des fleurs (etc.).
Suivez au tombeau notre soeur adorée.

Cast down flowers for the dead maiden!
As far as the grave, cast down flowers (etc.).
Follow our beloved sister to the grave.

On this simple text, supplemented by wordless vocalization, Berlioz composed an extended tableau derived from a scene which Garrick had introduced to provide an occasion for music. Berlioz outlined his formal, or at least his textural, intentions in the heading: he had adopted a similar process in the *Offertorium* ('Domine Jesu Christe') from his recent Requiem. Fugal and homophonic passages alternate against a monotone presented like a pedal, but intermittently; the reiterated pitch allowed Berlioz to exploit varied harmonic combinations without the restriction imposed by a continuous pedal.[1] However, there are significant formal differences between the *Convoi funèbre* and the *Offertoire*, summarized in Table 6.1.

This is the first section of the symphony which could be incorporated, without generic strain, into an opera; such processional movements are a common feature of theatre music in almost any period. However, during the *Convoi* the symphonic and dramatic actions are frozen, and the static nature of the material means that the purely musical aspects of the movement command attention. Perhaps this is why Berlioz adopted one of his favourite systematic designs, one which, here at least, is replete with ambiguity. The

Table 6.1 Comparison of *Offertoire* (Requiem) with *Convoi funèbre*

Offertoire (1837)	*Convoi funèbre* (1839)
D minor	E minor
Fugue subject tonally secure	Fugue subject tonally vagrant
Dominant 'pedal' with upper neighbour (a–b♭)	Tonic pedal, without other pitches
Steady rhythm not determined by words	Rhythmic pattern varied according to the words
Turn to major only at the end	Major reached half-way with return to minor at the end
No definable form	Sonata form

Convoi is the only movement in *Roméo et Juliette* that may be understood as a complete sonata form, but its textural procedures, notably ostinato and fugue, belong to other generic types. And the major divisions of the sonata do not coincide with those features of the musical topography most likely to affect a listener.

The sonata is the type with little or no development (see Table 6.2). Its thematic–tonal outline is clear, but a certain awkwardness resides in the brevity of the secondary material – and hence of the complementary key area – and in the length of the recapitulation. The latter is swollen by developmental transformations of the main idea; new counterpoints and a fugal stretto precede a version in the major (from bar 67), a change of mode which would more normally be withheld for the reprise of the secondary material.

The sonata design divides the movement asymmetrically, the reprise occurring near the 'negative' golden mean (bar 54).[2] But the symmetrical division into two nearly-equal halves has greater impact thanks to two synchronized (though not quite simultaneous) events: the exchange of roles between chorus and orchestra which begins almost tentatively in bar 65, and the change to the major mode (the new key-signature is at bar 68; the change occurs, however, with the fugue subject in the sopranos, bar 67). Another unexpected feature for a 'slow movement' sonata form is the length of the coda: if one experiences bar 67 as a mid-point, the movement has ten bars too many. But besides conforming with the Golden Section, this coda can be accounted for rhetorically, as one of the longest of Berlioz's recessional diminuendos.[3]

The movement is a portrayal of mourning; specifically, the mourning

Table 6.2 Sonata form in the *Convoi funèbre*

Bar	Key	Sonata section/[other]
1–39	e [b]	Exposition of principal material in fugue; modulation to
40–47	G	Secondary material (homophonic)
48–53	C–e	Retransition based on fugue subject
54–104	e	Recapitulation of principal material
[67–8]	E	[Exchange of vocal and instrumental roles]
105–13	E	Recapitulation of secondary material
114–42	E–e	Coda

particular to the wasteful loss of a young girl on the verge of matronhood. *We* of course know that Juliet is neither 'expirée' nor a 'vierge'; the expenditure of so much invention on Friar Lawrence's ruse may seem excessive. But the reactions of the Capulet family to Juliet's death are certainly moving (Shakespeare, Act IV scene 5) and in the symphony they substitute for a reaction to her real death for which the hectic closing stages of Berlioz's conception allow no time. The elegiac note, in short, is Shakespearean, even if the means to strike it are not.

The fugue subject is one of Berlioz's most remarkable inventions, conveying all the deep feeling with which the movement is imbued. Following the F major of the scherzo, its tonality is something of a shock, mitigated, perhaps, by the sense of its opening as a leading-note (quasi-dominant) b to c'.[4] The prolonged c' undermines any incipient sense of metre before a descent to the tonic (Ex. 6.1). The second limb of the subject is gropingly chromatic, its aspiration to return to b – a return not to hope but to a more adequate expression of grief – giving durational emphasis to pitches outside E minor (g♯, a♯). Then, as if cueing in the voices, the line skips to the octave e' and, reinforced by bassoons and oboe, makes gestures which still further undermine the tonal implications of the opening by strong suggestions of the subdominant, A minor, emphasized by *its* subdominant, D minor. The vocal interjections of the tonic 'pedal' are hardly enough to restore tonal order against this passionate declamation, which features the augmented second (c♯'–b♭) and diminished fourth (c♯'–f♮') traditional for musical mourning at least since Purcell. The ending returns ambiguously to b (pinched by c♮' and a♯), while the second voice enters for the subject in the dominant, B minor.[5] There is little Berlioz could add to the expressive intensity of this Bartókian

49

Ex. 6.1

elegy, and such growth as the movement does achieve results from its inexorable accumulation of texture. The intervals of the subject (semitone, diminished fourth) recur in the cello counterpoint to the viola answer, yet they tend to stabilize its tonality; grief is subsumed within the steady progress of ritual. The main rhetorical thrust, indeed, is away from the disordered mourning of the opening monody towards control. The third entry (bar 20) sets the chromatic ascent over a throbbing C♯, ten beats long, in the cellos, and the A minor propensity of bars 8–9 is confirmed at the expense of D minor (the B♭s are now clearly heard as 'Neapolitan' seconds within the key of A). Stability is also suggested by the lovely bassoon and viola counterpoint derived from the subject, and, with the fourth entry (first violins, end of bar 29), by the solidifying middle parts. Berlioz then moves to the traditional alternative key, the major mediant, for a homophonic passage; the swaying melody, slightly hypnotic in a good performance, is lightly counterpointed by oboe and bassoon.

The retransition is homophonic, and serves to stabilize the point of recapitulation in a manner directly contrary to sonata dynamics: instead of a new lease of life, a steady augmentation in the bass of the subject's C–B movement precedes a perfect cadence (bars 51–4). Over this clearly directed harmony a violin melody unfolds, taking bars 8–9 of the subject as the basis for meditation, at first diatonic (bar 49), then restoring the diminished fourth of mourning (51). This interval, however, is missing in the recapitulation which crushes the successive entries into a stretto. A continuation of the quaver pattern (second violins, flute) settles mesmerically into a two-note

Ex. 6.2

oscillation, slurred across the pulse, and overcoming the fugue: the bass sinks in a vast augmentation of the C to E descent from bars 2–3.

The exchange of material between orchestra and voices has the effect of reducing tension, but the beauty of Berlioz's writing for unaccompanied singers and the hypnotic effect of the orchestral pedal (now bell-chimes rather than psalmody) builds a different kind of intensity; the wordless soprano part recalls the Easter Hymn in *La Damnation*. The subject in the major retains only a residue of tonal ambiguity, for the inflections to C♯ minor (bars 72, 74–5) if anything strengthen E major. The interest of this long extension is maintained by texture: harmonizing the subject (bar 67), returning to fugue with vocalized counterpoint (79), then piling vocal entries at a bar's distance (95–7) with orchestral reinforcement (although the music remains strictly in three parts plus ostinato until the cadence at 103). The second theme is revealed as particularly appropriate for sighing voices, and the psalmody on E, previously heard against this theme as the sixth degree in G major, is finally established as the tonic.

The coda falls into two parts. The first is only the afterglow of the vocal fugue, but a textural division is made by silencing the voices. A further stabilization of the subject (compare Exx. 6.1 and 6.2) sets off from the third of the scale as well as the fifth, and contains only the lightest, most immediately neutralized, chromaticism. The later entries are poignantly deprived of the upbeat. The second part (or true coda) from bar 126 brings the pedal into line with the normal behaviour of a tocsin, a regular pealing in crotchets almost to the end.[6] The tremolo beneath wavers above the tonic, then descends a sixth (compare the subject, Ex.6.1) to fade almost arbitrarily on G♮: the root-position harmony of the hushed ending is violently animated to open the sixth movement.

No. 6 Roméo au tombeau

Roméo au tombeau des Capulets. Invocation: Réveil de Juliette. Joie délirante, désespoir; dernières angoisses et mort des deux amants.[7]

Romeo at the Capulet's tomb Invocation: Juliet's awakening. Delirious joy, despair; last agony and death of the lovers.

(1) *Allegro agitato e disperato* ($\downarrow$ = 144)

In this movement the music is purely instrumental, yet almost purely representational; some of it could accompany a mime enacted virtually in real time. The astonishing quality of the music clearly owes much to Berlioz's visual memories of *Romeo and Juliet* in the theatre. Quite apart from the first performance (see above, p. 7), he relates in his *Mémoires* that in 1829 he stumbled into a rehearsal of the play, with Harriet apparently dead in Romeo's arms, and fled in anguish.[8] No other part of *Roméo et Juliette* has aroused so much controversy (see Chapters 8 and 9).

The movement is subdivided three times by tempo markings, but to the listener, despite its relative brevity, it appears to have six sections. The stuttering violence of the opening may parallel Romeo's frantic efforts to open the tomb; more importantly, it is a metaphor of his mental state. Conflicting emotions appear in the disruptive tonal scheme: the first period embraces directional thrusts to F and B♭ major within E minor (cadence in bar 16: Ex. 6.3). The rhythm is equally disruptive, regular short phrases giving way to triple units (bars 11–13). A unison D ends the domain of E minor, but the meaning of its resolution on C♯ only gradually becomes clear: the goal is not yet A major, but C♯ minor. The second period (18–33) uses similar, rather than identical, short motives, and its disruptive ascent is more directed, reaching an extended D♯–G♯ progression before the curt final gesture sends the middle register down to b♯ and the harmonic context stabilizes as the dominant of C♯.

Change follows in every parameter, despite the absence of any new tempo direction; the next fifteen bars are all unmeasured fermatas. Time is suspended.[9] The passage suggests the awe-struck Romeo apprehending the cold darkness of the tomb. Each chord is differently scored, but alternate ones repeat the dominant of C♯; the neighbouring harmonies ('N' in Ex. 6.3) become increasingly remote until the mystic ambiguity of the half-diminished

Ex. 6.3

seventh (bar 44) leaves the oboe suspended. The finality of the dominant is enhanced by a minor ninth in the flute.

(2) Invocation *Largo* ($\flat$ = 132)

The second tempo consists mainly of an 'aria' for Romeo, in the tenor register, his voice darker than in the *Scène d'amour* through the absence of cellos; a unison of four bassoons and horn is qualified by the nasal cor anglais, previously Juliet's instrument. The off-beat accent of the accompaniment recalls the other tomb scene which Berlioz associated with this play.[10] The melody, articulate even in despair, falls into a complex but clear periodization, and is drawn through some potentially remote regions before falling, with a climactic D major chord, to a C♯ minor cadence.[11] Romeo's wordless 'aria' is suggested by lines from the play (V.3):

> O my love, my wife,
> Death, that hath suck'd the honey of thy breath,
> Hath had no power yet upon thy beauty:
> Thou art not conquer'd; beauty's ensign yet
> Is crimson in thy lips and in thy cheeks . . .

At its conclusion, where he drinks a phial of poison, the sinking figure in the cellos (bar 71) is an impressive metaphor for his impending dissolution.

At this point in the Garrick dénouement Juliet wakes up. Berlioz's response to this near-supernatural event (as it must seem to Romeo) is a comparable disruption of normality: melodic and harmonic events fail to coincide. The 'aria' sinks to a low c♯, but the line has no harmonic support, only its simultaneous contradiction by the cellos' G♮ (their written-out trill to A♭ fails to attain the harmonically more rational goal, A♭/G♯). There are four fermatas before the next tempo-marking, and the sense of being outside notated time is comparable to the passage before the Invocation. Above the G♮, the clarinet creeps in almost inaudibly; its utterance gradually takes shape as Juliet's theme from the *Scène d'amour*. Between her phrases Romeo's cellos and basses respond, first with a languid gesture almost implying a C major tonality, then with a move, at last, to G♯ then D, forming an outline of the dominant of A. Melodic and harmonic factors are about to converge as the section closes into a cadence; its tonic is the first chord of the following tempo, which enters explosively, topped by an added sixth.

(3) *Allegro vivace ed appassionato assai* ($\downharpoonright = 144$)

The metronome indicates the same speed as the opening, but the material has a totally different character. The music is still disruptive, particularly in its reluctance to commit itself to any clear harmonic bass (in which it takes a characteristic of Berlioz's music to extremes).[12] There is, however, no doubt of its adherence to A major, and when motives define themselves after the change to $\frac{6}{8}$ they are clearly recognizable as 'Romeo's declaration' from the *Scène d'amour* (in both C♯ and C major: No. 3, bars 146, 172; No. 6, bars 108, 124). The orchestration is strident, with cornets dominating; the rhythms again break free of the barline. Climax mounts on climax, but no goal emerges; indeed, like the ball music, the rhythmically frenzied music seems in danger of becoming frozen in terms of pitch.

For the third time the music breaks down, again with marked use of silence

Ex. 6.4

(there are four further fermatas before the movement ends and several other measured silences). The barlines are merely notional when Berlioz suddenly superimposes $\frac{3}{4}$ and $\frac{4}{4}$ metres, with a dismal moan from the trombones notated (though not audibly) in $\frac{6}{8}$. And atonality seems imminent when a bass arpeggio moves down by giant strides of a fourth (from bar 169): b♭, f♮, c♮, G♮, before sinking a third to the dominant pitch, E (Ex. 6.4). At this point the string ostinato between b♭''' and d♭''' moves up a semitone to outline the dominant minor ninth in A (bar 183: the treble reaches d''', and the violas reach f♮'', the minor ninth).[13] Harmonically, this is a perfect cadence, but the texture remains hopelessly disruptive and the principal melodic pitches obstinately remain around c♯ (the former d♭), in various registers. Romeo's life drains away in a double neighbour-note figure in the double basses (G♯/B♭ surrounding A), which anticipates the death of Juliet moments later. First, however, the unhappy girl seizes his dagger, and with a wordless invocation set as instrumental recitative (violins) of violently disruptive character, she stabs herself (bar 211).[14] The reiteration of the B♭–A movement in the bass in slow motion is grimmer than silence: the oboe, *pppp*, intones three notes grouped chromatically round the dominant and three round the tonic, then the main pitches, E–A, drip gloomily from the cellos.[15] Berlioz marks a final fermata before the finale begins on the same modally indeterminate harmony.

No. 7 Finale

La foule accourt au cimetière –	The crowd rushes to the cemetery –
Rixe des Capulets et des Montagus.	Strife between Capulets and Montagues.
Récitatif et Air du père Laurence.	Recitative and aria of Frair Lawrence.
Serment de Réconciliation.	Oath of reconciliation.

[For the text see Appendix 2]

The finale, which Berlioz called the only scene 'in the realm of opera or oratorio', could indeed be staged in every respect but the addition of the prologue chorus which has no place in a theatrical rendering of the scene. Nevertheless, the interpretation of the drama is hardly less original than in the instrumental scenes, for the reconciliation, as already pointed out, takes place under the aegis of the Church rather than the secular power. Originally Berlioz included some Shakespearean lines concerning the erection of statues to the young lovers.[16] These created a slackening of musical tension (corresponding to an element of poetic banality), and were rightly removed following condemnation in the press (see Chapter 7). The finale falls into clearly defined sections:

(1) *Allegro* ($\bullet$ = 100), then *Molto più lento* ($\bullet$ = 112). Picking up from the ambiguous, but A-centred, end of No. 6, the brass fanfare represents a Shakespearean 'alarum', the strings the bustling of running feet.[17] Over a throbbing pedal the voices enter severally, piling up a major chord on 'Roméo!' before breaking into crude imitation. The bodies are discovered and over a deep sustained A♭ the families are briefly united in shock: 'Morts tous les deux, et leur sang fume encore'. Their lament brings only an open resolution, on the dominant of C minor.[18]

(2) *Allegro non troppo* ($\bullet$ = 144, with much tempo variation). Lawrence intervenes to unveil the mystery. His narrative brings the first operatic vocal recitative, nearer in style to the instrumental recitatives in Nos. 3 and 6 than to the Prologue's psalmody. This section is centred on C minor, although an immediate turn towards E♭ (oboe, bar 50) anticipates the eventual key of his aria. His words are punctuated by choral reaction, to news of the marriage, then to the notion of befriending the other family: their curses impel Lawrence into a sustained Allegro ($\bullet$ = 84) of measured declamation, almost an aria but for the continual, non-periodic modulation. The urgent accompaniment, complemented by a chromatic sigh in the violins, underlines a steady melodic ascent to a first climax in the remote key of G♭ (bar 83) as he tells of Juliet pouring out her woes. In shame, his voice dropping by semitones, Lawrence tells of the potion.[19] The tonality is still more ambiguous, but touches, at the choral murmur 'Un breuvage!' (bar 99), on a later goal, B minor. To a continuing accompaniment of growing intensity, and with a gradual increment of sustained and syncopated wind, Lawrence gathers strength as he outlines the full extent of the tragedy. Beyond the C minor cadence (bar 131) he sinks to a low A at 'la vérité' (the truth); the stupefied families mutter 'Married!', as the implications sink in.

(3) Lawrence's aria in E♭ ('Pauvres enfants'; *Larghetto sostenuto*: $\bullet$ = 54) is a moment of reflection on the tragedy set in a tone of noble simplicity, enriched by subtle chromaticism. Inspired by a grandiose vision, Lawrence stands outside the action, prophesying that Verona will be most famed as the home of the star-crossed pair. In the *Allegro non troppo* ($\bullet$ = 144) Lawrence returns to the present: are not the families ashamed? The dramatic change (bar 190) matches a tonal leap from E♭ to B major, the eventual final key, established by a humming ostinato on the violins. The vocal style is declamatory, but this proves to be the second part of an aria of magnificently controlled rhetoric. The expected closure (approached from *c*. bar 220) is interrupted; this section of the aria does not resume, and is never cadenced. Instead Lawrence

pronounces the verdict of heaven: 'Pour que là-haut ma vengeance pardonne' (bar 229: *Andante maestoso*: $\downarrow$ = 58).

(4) *Allegro* ($\downarrow$ = 116, as in No. 1). At first Lawrence only triggers the families' reflexes; having learned nothing, they revert to the music of the introduction, first as a vocal fugato. Although compressed, it reaches the same harmonic goal, the dominant of D (bar 263; compare No. 1, bar 43). Lawrence commands them to silence. The D minor region visited here is sombre in comparison to the abrasive B minor and his chromatic sigh from section 2 is extended to cover more than two octaves (from bars 266–7). He turns directly to God; unusually for a prayer, the tempo doubles. This superb paragraph (bar 296, 'Grand Dieu qui voit au fond de l'âme') surges from D major to the crest of a wave in B major, reversing the tonal trend of the previous passage but in the major mode (b–d: D–B). He is strengthened by an aspiring bass figure and by a ripe entry of brass at the climax.[20] This declamation is melodically formed, constituting the final section of the aria, a point Berlioz makes by repeating the last strain (somewhat abbreviated, from bar 336; compare bar 304) with the gradual addition of the choruses in long suspended syllables ('O__ Juliette, O__ Roméo'). As Lawrence reaches his triumphant assertion the chorus, to a continuation of the ostinato, suddenly looks at itself: 'Dieu! quel prodige étrange'; their surprise is expressed in winding sequences to a temporary repose on the dominant of G major (bars 364–70), a melodic curve suited to the evocation of heavenly tears.

(5) 'Oath' (*Andante un poco maestoso*, $\downarrow$. = 54). It remains only to seal their new-found compassion with friendship. Lawrence leads with a grandly Meyerbeerian paragraph animated by Berlioz's lively accompaniment and redeemed from banality by its transparent sincerity and by finely controlled modulations.[21] A two–note figure is gradually introduced in the violins: at first it appears occasionally in isolation, then two then three statements appear in succession, and with the repetition of the oath by the chorus (bar 404) it springs forth as an enlivening ostinato.[22]

It is worth noting, in these resplendent final pages, how economical Berlioz is in building the climax and true goal of some 100 minutes' music, fulfilling the 'law of the crescendo' which he identified in justification of the design of Beethoven's Ninth.[23] The percussion (now the full group of bass drum, cymbals, and timpani) is introduced occasionally, to punctuate (but in *piano*). The men's voices lead and the women are added only at bar 409 with a kind of descant. At bar 419 the whole ensemble drops, eventually to *pianissimo*, a dynamic springboard used again when they reach the mysterious falling sequence from bar 427, which Berlioz harmonizes with considerable ingenuity. The main verse begins a third statement (bar 437); only here are all the forces used in a *forte* or *fortissimo*, with full (but often *pp*) percussion support. This proves to be a rounding-off and after eight bars it breaks into powerful quasi-sacred diatonic harmony resembling climactic moments in Berlioz's Requiem and Te Deum.[24] Thus the musical idiom bears out the dramatic interpretation whereby the reconciliation is achieved through the sign of the cross.

7

A view from 1839 by Stephen Heller

Stephen Heller's review of *Roméo et Juliette* appeared in two parts in the *Revue et Gazette musicale* in December 1839 and in five parts in the *Neue Zeitschrift für Musik*, Leipzig, in January–February 1840.[1] Heller was not the only sympathetic reviewer of the first performances (see Chapter 8), but he was the best-qualified musician, Wagner aside, to report on them. Schumann, as editor of the *Neue Zeitschrift*, had reviewed the *Symphonie fantastique* favourably in 1835, and the present article aided the growth of German interest in Berlioz upon which he capitalized in the 1840s and 1850s. I have indicated short cuts by [. . .]. They consist mainly of extracts from the libretto or factual descriptions of instrumentation, unnecessary here; a few contain allusive matter without adding to the argument. The leisurely style of reviews in specialized nineteenth-century periodicals has necessitated some compression in the translation which, however, affects style rather then substance. All the notes are mine.

To Robert Schumann, at Leipzig, Paris, December 1839

My dear friend: [. . .] I would rather send you Berlioz's symphony itself than a dry analysis; that way you could hear and see, with perfect clarity, what criticism can only hint at. [. . .] What the public most wants of art is novelty and originality; yet on experiencing plenty of both it reacts badly because its own understanding is incomplete. Perversely, it blames the author rather than itself; it asks for works newly minted from basic principles, which at the same time fulfil its own routine expectations. [. . .] Berlioz's symphony needs no more defence from such prejudice than his other works. All new, original, bold music must be repeated until no-one finds it new, bold, or original. This is no paradox; have not many listeners, including honest musicians, trembled in the presence of Beethoven's Choral symphony? Because it showed greater freedom, inspiration, genius than ever, it was declared bizarre, obscure, disorderly, barbarous! Yet it was admitted to contain very beautiful sections;

a pity one had to work hard to find them, in comparison with his earlier works – forgetting that the D major symphony [No. 2] was formerly compared to its disadvantage with Haydn and Mozart.

My enthusiasm for the 'Ninth' won't make me despise Beethoven's earlier music; nor will my admiration for Berlioz's symphonies desensitize me to other masterpieces. But to grasp his new forms, to become familiar with them and fully understand his merits, needs work. We are no longer frightened by the savage and fantastical finale of Beethoven's Eighth, nor [do we] recoil from the dissonant C in the transition from the Scherzo to the finale of the [Fifth] symphony in C minor. Forewarned, we enjoy them because they are fine, authentic, captivating; we don't ask first whether or not they contain innovations.[2] Yet when we come to Berlioz, people are still anxious to know if such and such a procedure has been used before; and every time one honestly admits that it hasn't, our *connoisseur* shakes his head knowingly and says (or thinks) that no good will come of it. But that earlier symphonies managed without programmes or librettos is no reason for carrying on in the same way through eternity. [. . .]

What intrinsic objection is there to a dramatic symphony with chorus, solo voices, and prologue in 'harmonic recitative'? I can only think of one: the problem of evoking something visible without the complex apparatus of the stage and the magic of theatrical perspective. But shouldn't we applaud the courage of an artist who works this miracle through music alone – bearing in mind that in opera music plays, or should play, the leading role? Is not reaching the same goal with fewer means what we call progress? For me, adding a prologue to a programme symphony is one of Berlioz's best notions, especially when he not only needs to get general ideas across, as in his earlier symphonies (march to execution, ball scene, Sabbath night, pilgrims' march), but the connected scenes of a sublime tragedy. If his orchestral movements are to be understood in the way he meant, he has to make his intentions clear.

A word on Berlioz's 'descriptive system' may be timely. To my mind, Berlioz never asks of music more effects than it can supply. People have always admitted that music can express pleasure, sorrow, love, sadness, fear, majesty; do we need to debar Berlioz from translating such feelings into sounds and harmonies? Don't opera audiences often exclaim: 'that oboe phrase is perfect for the siren'; or, when the high priest enters: 'Don't those trombones make a stunning effect?' and so forth? And they are right; we can't refute the evidence of their ears, even if we find such routine associations (two oboes with sirens, trombones with a high priest, the clarinet with the misguided vestal) somewhat risible.[3] And these *topoi* are perfectly natural; dramatic action harnessed to imagination justifies their use. So the Prologue of Berlioz's new symphony brings the listener into line with the composer's creative thought; it helpfully defines the dramatic structure by summarizing the tragic events; and it not only explains the musical sections but translates, as it were for the eyes, the action which needs so much apparatus in the theatre. Didn't Shakespeare put his plays on in a barn? And wasn't the excitement of the dramatic illusion enough to make one forget that four bare walls represented now a garden bower, now the décor of a great house? Admittedly, for public understanding, dramatic scenes transcribed into music instead of being presented by singers represent a still greater novelty: the likely reaction is: 'What does it mean? How can combinations of timbre and pitch convey feelings? What links a nun and two bassoons? How is the casting of bullets in *Der Freischütz* helped by a minor third held by two flutes?[4] We want words, nothing but words; we don't need music to colour or reinforce their expression'. Very good! but today, with Berlioz's symphony, they say 'We want music, nothing but music; we don't need words to display its charms'.

There are fine tragedies without music, fine symphonies without words, and fine operas; so why not accept dramatic symphonies as well, even if they are an innovation? Every genre was new once; a permanent statute of exclusion would have lost us much that we enjoy the most. But these are just preliminary reflections: now to the analysis.

The B minor introduction to Berlioz's symphony might be called a short overture. Imagine a fugal Allegro which grows more and more lively and rumbustious until a grandly effective fortissimo in D major, after which it gradually decays, as if anger and passion were quelled: a strong, truthful picture of the bitter fighting between Capulets and Montagues. As the tumult fades away a grandly powerful trombone phrase marks the intervention and orders of the Prince. People have quibbled about this as if it were a political speech; but critics who won't discuss it as a princely intervention allow it at least to be that of three trombones and an ophicleide.[5] Either way, it is a strong and effective utterance in recitative style. The original fugato reappears, broken as if expressing muttered threats; then it disappears completely. The semi-chorus of altos, tenors and basses begins a harmonic recitative enhanced by intriguing orchestral interjections.

When the story reaches the love scene, there is a well-placed song ['Strophes'] reflecting on the charm of first love. [. . .] The melody and accompaniment belong among Berlioz's most intimate and touching inspirations. The final phrase, 'dans le ciel', is given in full, sustained harmonies supported by the chorus. The obbligato cello of the second strophe is particularly effective; it supports the voice part by an independent line, or by decorating it, as if with a floral crown. The prologue continues with an invocation to Queen Mab, the dream fairy, a vocal Scherzino in F major ($\frac{2}{4}$, Allegro leggiero). [. . .] You could go a long way without finding anything wittier or more evocative; each note is a spark of genius. The flutes [*recte* flute and piccolo] shadow the melody with ghostly fluttering and chattering, and the cellos complete a delicious pizzicato accompaniment mingled with legato bowing. The choral echo of the soloist's words is truly original. The Scherzino vanishes without warning, like a will o'the wisp skimming away on Dr Faustus's cloak, and the prologue continues a little further, ending with two vibrant orchestral chords. Many listeners found it too long; but I can't condone skipping the preface of a book to get on with the story. An intelligent preface helps you to understand the argument, and can itself form an independent and complete work, like this summary of Berlioz's symphony.

The first orchestral piece follows, its programme: 'Romeo alone – Distant sounds of the ball and concert – Grand feast at Capulet's'. I am reluctant to transcribe these lines, which could be used to argue for or against descriptive music; but, I repeat, there is nothing in this programme to inhibit musicality; it is hardly the first time music has been used to evoke the misery of a wandering, love-struck dreamer, the crescendo of a dance orchestra, and an actual festivity. The movement begins with a plaintive legato on unaccompanied violins, not itself quite a melody, more the introduction to the one which emerges next on oboes and clarinets, developed fully and richly with violins soon adding to its intensity in graceful alternation with the woodwind. Pure lyricism is interrupted by a sudden allegro and a lively short phrase for clarinets and bassoons promises a piquant contrast, but it does not last. It is followed by a short Larghetto confided to the solo oboe, decorated with an accompaniment as light as it is original. This is not one of my favourite passages; [. . .] although it finally acquires a more passionate character, its charm is of the Italian kind.[6] With the Allegro the lively phrase already mentioned seems to get rapidly nearer, clearer, and more vigorous; the whole orchestra gets hold of it, then the violins take it up with an effusion of joy and clamour. The wind instruments follow on, while the violins play a smooth counterpoint and the remaining strings provide an accompaniment in broken quavers [bar 187]; this combination has the effect of distant music heard from the street. Then the forces seem to double in size; the orchestra takes hold of the main theme with irresistible verve and incredible allure [bar 226] while the oboes, horns, bassoons and trombones unite in a broad fortissimo phrase, already sketched [bar 207] by bassoons and trombones.[7] [. . .] However, a legato figure against a fugato in bassoons, oboes, flutes and clarinets, lets us breathe again before an immense crescendo restores the radiant but irresponsible glitter of the ball.[8] The allegro keeps returning to the sonority of its main theme, altered in style, and there is too much detail to describe it fully. This spirited piece won the public over and finished amid an outbreak of cheering.

The ball is over; the Capulet chorus leaves, humming the dance-tunes and commending the generosity of their host; here I think Berlioz wanted to satirize the *dilettanti*.[9] They change the metre to $\frac{6}{8}$, but in doing so they produce a variation which has a charm of its own; this, equally, may represent Berlioz's intention. [. . .] This double chorus is very pretty, but I prefer the lovely accompaniment of strings, two horns, and flutes for its marvellous harmonic combinations on long-held notes, perfectly balancing the exuberant song of the youths. One horn solo [presumably bar 35] has a specially curious and delicious effect.

The chorus of Capulets drifts away, and the garden scene begins. This Adagio had less success than the preceding piece at the first performance, but at the second it attracted something like the sympathy it deserves. [. . .] Nothing is more profoundly felt than this Adagio; to me it hardly matters that it is 'about' the love of Romeo and Juliet rather than some other passion. What have we to do with Juliet *confiding her love to the night*, as the prologue tells us, with Romeo suddenly revealing himself to her, and with their happiness or anxiety? This is mere fiction, while the music is incontrovertibly real. Its melodies penetrate to the wellsprings of emotion, arouse a thousand diverse sensations, and move us to tears! I agree with those who recognized the extreme beauty of this Adagio but felt it nevertheless to be over-extended; if, that is, anything so fine can go on too long. Berlioz has the rare gift of enlivening an Adagio by variation of metre and by introducing a sort of recitative; I don't know any slow movement as dramatic as this. The recitative (or song in recitative style, confided to the cellos) intervenes in a short *allegro agitato*. [. . .] I seem to have said nothing about the theme or the modulations, of striking novelty in all Berlioz but especially here; nor have I commented on the orchestration. How to find words for such harmonic progressions, such admirable *cantilena* for violins, oboe, or particularly cor anglais? Certainly this Adagio is a devastating response to the critics of Berlioz who claim that he lacks melodic inspiration. [. . .] Berlioz does not expose his melody naked; it is artistically covered, though not concealed, by delicate tissue; this is why people suggest he fails. I confess that one passage in this Adagio seems to me dispensable. Towards the end the clarinets ascend in thirds, followed by the violins; this lasts three bars, after which comes an extraordinary two-part cello solo, unaccompanied. This weird idea recurs several times in fifteen bars. Several wind instruments take up the figure in thirds, but the cellos persist in their bizarre solo.[10] I think I have represented Berlioz fairly, but while I admit the combination is original, it lacks charm. But let us pass over this minor flaw: the theme returns, broken up in a decidedly piquant manner, and this masterly Adagio dies away with a melody seemingly murmured by mysterious voices.

No. 4: Scherzo, in F major, $\frac{3}{8}$ Prestissimo, which conveys nothing of the barely imaginable originality of this movement. I would rather say no more than that its subject is Queen Mab, or the Dream Fairy. If you want more words, you only realize their inadequacy in the face of this astonishing scherzo, which belongs wholly in the realm of dreams and fairyland, and whose effect is irresistible. [. . .] What can I say about this musical evocation of supernatural creatures who turn the laws of nature upside down? Perhaps Berlioz discovered the manuscript in the same place as the little antique cymbals which he deploys to delicious effect. It is rumoured that he found them in the ruins of Herculaneum and brought them back from his triumphant pilgrimage to Rome.[11] [. . .] Berlioz rightly allows free rein to his fertile imagination and his fantastic caprice. The misty and evasive theme passes from one instrument to another, always varied, always interesting, now naive, now severe, by turns ebullient, grotesque, mocking, languorous, energetic, witty, bellicose, galant, morose, brimming over with malice, spirit, poetry! in short – this scherzo ends the first part of the symphony. I have tried to give you an idea of it, and I have failed, as does every critic who has written and is writing about it. [. . .][12]

The second part of Berlioz's symphony begins with another prologue in recitative still more remarkable than the first. Certain passages provoked my particular admiration: *Romeo utters a delirious cry*, and the accompaniment offers us a sharp exclamation; further on, the basses sing several lines [from 'Les deux familles ennemies' to 'haine héréditaire'], to which the accompaniment alternating two trombones and two bassoons contains very fine harmony. Shortly afterwards the choral prologue ends most touchingly with a final line: 'Which, alas, spilled so much blood, so many tears'.[13]

No. 5 [. . .] This piece exudes deep feeling, unutterable sorrow. On the words 'Cast down flowers for the dead virgin!' a rich harmony is marvellously combined with the orchestral march, an effect then reproduced, to equal effect, when their roles are exchanged.[14] The sublimity of this movement eluded the first audience, but at the second performance an impression was made and rewarded with vigorous applause. Undoubtedly it will eventually be considered, as it deserves, among the loveliest things in the symphony. Nevertheless, I wish Berlioz had resisted including, after the march, ten dull bars of ecclesiastical psalmody: *Requiem aeternam dona eis*, etc., if only because it jars to hear the singers of the poetic 'Throw flowers' immediately turn to mumbling a monotonous plainsong.[15] After this short and priestly prayer, quite unconnected to the march, there is a reprise of the fugue theme and the piece ends in a fresh and striking way.

No. 6. The programme explains the subdivision of this orchestral movement into several sections: [see Chapter 6]. The opening *allegro agitato e disperato* (E minor, in duple time) fully justifies this direction. Otherwise it has to be said that the explanatory text is absolutely necessary to avoid misunderstanding this passionate and sorrowful music; unless one is totally engaged by the tragic situation, the music could be mistaken for a rehearsal of an exceptionally dramatic opera performed by the orchestra alone to an empty stage. You may take this both as a reproach and a eulogy. Such energetic and sombre music, faithfully characterizing a tragic catastrophe, must arouse painful feelings.

The gaps, as in the orchestral contribution to an opera, cannot in this case be filled by what one sees. Yet this music so clearly expresses the dramatic qualities of the situation, which it clothes in the most vividly striking colours, that it must inspire in the spectator the desire for a physical complement, and regret for the absence of scenery and staging. Even without its title *Invocation*, the Largo in C♯ minor is of great beauty, a lovely *cantilena* on cor anglais, two horns and two bassoons, with violas and cello accompaniment, and an intermittent *pianissimo* drum roll to increase the noble elevation of its sentiment. A clarinet solo, cut into by viola and bass figures, represents the plaintive voice of Juliet as she revives from her stupor; the full orchestra explodes into an *allegro appassionato* (A major, $\frac{4}{4}$) using the motive of the garden scene, first within the $\frac{4}{4}$ metre, then back in $\frac{6}{8}$, but changed to express delirious joy, then too soon harrowing anguish: after the deep feelings of the Adagio and the vivid joy of the Allegro, the same motive appears broken, harsh, breathless, and virtually unrecognizable.

After a few orchestral bars the finale begins with a choral phrase of musical beauty and incomparable drama, worthy of the greatest: enough to establish Berlioz as a master. The melody at 'Morts tous les deux . . . ' is weighed down by despair. Then Friar Lawrence, in a measured recitative, explains the catastrophe. This movement, as much aria in character as recitative, has many attractions, but it would produce a stronger effect if one did not already know the events it narrates.[16] This objection is easily answered by an appeal to the effectiveness of the *music*, but the sheer dramatic excitement Berlioz impresses on his composition makes it all the more necessary to avoid the snare of tautology. Repetition is a basic element in music; but dramatic dialogue, action, must happen quickly, and the detailed narration of something the audience already knows lowers its emotional temperature and makes it impatient. Hence this grandly declaimed scene for Lawrence may never be appreciated as it deserves. The following aria in E♭ is of the finest workmanship, but it also lacks dramatic grip, at least until the vigorous exclamation: 'Where are they now, these fierce enemies?' The B major Allegro and the Andante maestoso are of marvellous quality. The violas and basses growl sombrely, while the soft and extended harmonies of the wind alternately grow and diminish [from bar 229].

The Montagues and Capulets return to the fugato of the Introduction. Each side reproaches the other with its bloody misdeeds. [. . .] The stirring up of anger is depicted with considerable force until Lawrence's violent expostulation: 'Non, lâches, perfides! . . . '. His 'Pouvez-vous sans remords . . . ' is a touching and persuasive response, as is the next section: 'Grand Dieu! qui voit au fond de l'âme' [bar 296]. I advise you, dear Schumann, to sit in a dark corner when you hear this symphony in Germany, so as not to display your tears at: 'Touchez ces coeurs sombres et durs!' The final part of this aria is periodically interrupted by the chorus, whose utterances are gradually filled with remorse as if the rough husk hugging inveterate hatred to their hearts splits under the influence of deeply touching harmonies. For the involuntary submission of these fierce enemies to an imperative – expiation of the tragic death of the lovers – the great composer finds powerful accents to convey the sublimity of his thought, the inexpressible truth of feeling. The choruses register surprise at their unexpected conversion ('Dieu! quel prodige étrange!'), then the musical character changes abruptly. At the eloquently resonating chord of G major [bar 366], I seem to see dark clouds dividing; a visionary blue sky fills me with renewed life and hope. The melody, by a seductive transition, reaches the key of B major;[17] then comes the grandiose oath of reconciliation. The priest's majestic solo, most noble in style, is accompanied by wind instruments while the violins have an effect of great originality: an interjection of two slurred notes at irregularly but steadily reduced intervals between each entry, finally amplified by double basses completing the line with cadences.

In the end orchestra and choruses unite in a general fortissimo. The developing violin figure now fills the whole bar, and the chorus repeats the formula of the oath, partly in unison, partly in a very lovely harmonization.

The role of Lawrence is isolated and continues alongside the chorus.[18] Here the melodic invention seems rather weak after the earlier marvels; at the end there is some rhythmic confusion, all the more striking after the splendid choral oath which resembles a great national hymn. Its reprise follows with redoubled vigour, thanks to the sudden entry of wind instruments, timpani, and cymbals. Berlioz has managed to cap his extraordinarily effective fortissimo by having the orchestra and chorus give out the three beats of the $\frac{9}{8}$ bar antiphonally [bar 446 onwards].

I must frankly admit that I would have liked the symphony to end here.[19] Berlioz shouldn't have made the chorus re-enter with hesitation, even doubt and residual hatred, postponing the definitive reconciliation. He no more than I would miss the passage, admirable in itself, where the two parties again urge each another towards concord ('Allons, frères, jurons!'). During a chromatic scale of clarinets, flutes, oboes and cellos, the horns and timpani hold the B in syncopated notes: again, this is all very well in itself but the general effect would improve if the whole piece ended with the powerful chords of the oath. Finally a somewhat too extended orchestral phrase serves to complete this immense composition.

My review, dear friend, shows you how difficult it is to analyse such a large, complicated work; it would have been easier to write a book than a letter. I only wish the railway ran from Leipzig to Paris, so that you could come at once and hear this symphony yourself; for its miraculous performance fully justifies the European reputation of the Conservatoire musicians.

My earlier irritation with the public only applies to certain passages, such as the prologue and the funeral procession. The friends and admirers of Berlioz otherwise took every opportunity to congratulate him. At the second performance, in particular, he was applauded with such enthusiasm that he could scarcely master his feelings. It is a real joy for the friends of art to see such an advance in public taste, and to witness a man of genius striding boldly forth on a glorious path away from the prosaic and commonplace, from sterile routine and theory.

Farewell, my friend; a thousand compliments to our dear family concerts, our music societies, our vocal reunions and virtuoso quartet players, all good things readily enjoyed in Germany; yet you should envy my hearing Berlioz's symphony five times already (including rehearsals), and again next Sunday, the 15th. For my part I envy your future happiness in offering Berlioz and his symphony the hospitality they deserve.

Yours ever. Stephen Heller.

PS This letter is going off later than I expected. By now the third Berlioz concert has taken place; this last hearing confirms everything I have said about this great work. The concert included a revival of two movements from the *Harold* symphony (the first, and the Pilgrims' March, which the Conservatoire audience particularly likes and which was repeated by general demand). I must pass over in silence the excellent performance of the orchestra; and as for the role of Father Lawrence in the new symphony, I wish that Berlioz could always find a singer as superior and intelligent as M. Alizard, a young artist with a brilliant future.

8

Performance and reception: 1839 and beyond

Following its first three performances, *Roméo et Juliette* suffered an immediate erosion of integrity. There were only six more complete performances in Berlioz's lifetime, none of them in France; meanwhile he split off various sections, himself inaugurating the practice (which continues today) of performing the three main instrumental movements as a triptych.[1] By far the commonest extract in Berlioz's concerts, however, was No. 2 by itself; only very recently has No. 6, although purely orchestral, been added to conductors' selections.[2] Excerpts were standard fare in Berlioz's concerts in Paris and abroad, and he was frequently able to claim a major success from these performances in his travel memoirs (intended for publication) and in personal letters.[3]

Integrity is a quality even some friendly critics suggest that *Roméo et Juliette* always lacked. But its dismemberment did not result from any perception on Berlioz's part that it was a miscellany like *Lélio* or *Tristia*: by performing separate movements, he was treating *Roméo et Juliette* no differently from his other symphonic works. As a promoter, he had to appeal to his audience while avoiding excessive outlay; performance of the instrumental movements was an obvious way of reminding the public of the work's existence without the cost of soloists and chorus.[4] As early as August 1840, therefore, while introducing the new *Symphonie funèbre* to audiences, he performed the *Fête chez Capulet*, and in December he mounted the first four movements in a concert at the Conservatoire.[5] Nos. 5 and 6 having been relatively unsuccessful, and No. 7 being expensive (with additional chorus), they were conveniently omitted in favour of the *Symphonie fantastique*. 'Strophes' from the Prologue appeared separately in print as early as 1839.[6] It figured in a concert in Brussels, during Berlioz's first venture abroad in September 1842, and with No. 2 it was the first part performed in Germany, at Dresden where Berlioz was to score many triumphs, on 17 February 1843. On this tour, the largest selection was again Nos. 1-4 inclusive, in Berlin on 23 April. The fourth complete performance took place on Berlioz's second voyage to Germany, in

Vienna on 2 January 1846. Another was given on 17 April in Prague and two more followed in St Petersburg during 1847. The next (20 November 1852) formed part of Liszt's 'Berlioz Week' at Weimar; the last was at Detmold during 1853, but in Berlioz's absence. Only the last two complete performances followed publication, and in 1858, having recently published a second, revised edition of the full score, Berlioz gave away his autograph to Jean-Georges Kastner.[7]

Although during his second German campaign Berlioz was composing *La Damnation de Faust*, he revised *Roméo et Juliette* extensively between the Vienna and Prague performances. In his *Mémoires* he records his reactions to early criticism:

... none of the experts who praised or denounced my work condescended to show me even one of the specific flaws which I was later to correct ...

Ernst's secretary Frankoski in Vienna pointed out a weakness in the ending of the Queen Mab Scherzo; it was too sudden, so I composed the present coda instead. I think it was d'Ortigue who advised me to make a cut in Friar Lawrence's narrative, to its great advantage ... All other modifications, additions and cuts were my own initiative, after seeing the effect the work made as a whole and in its details at performances in Paris, Berlin, Vienna and Prague.[8]

Berlioz may be forgiven his heat, but memory or *amour propre* played him false: in 1839 several well-disposed critics did point out specific imperfections, and Berlioz acted on at least some of their advice. Admittedly not much benefit could be obtained from a report like Wagner's to the Dresden *Abendzeitung* early in 1840: he allows Berlioz to be 'an absolute exception to long-established rules', but in *Roméo et Juliette* 'there are so many examples of tastelessness and so many artistic blemishes, ranged side by side with passages of pure genius, that I could not help wishing that Berlioz had shown it before the performance to a man like Cherubini, who would certainly have known how to remove a large number of its ugly distortions . . . '.[9] But those who mentioned it unanimously condemned the short 'Requiem aeternam' at the end of the *Convoi funèbre*; Berlioz dropped it, possibly before the second performance. Several critics suggested that both the *Scène d'amour* and finale were too long; Berlioz eventually responded to these criticisms as well. The finale was reduced in two places. The Friar's speech, as Stephen Heller observed, was tautological anyway, and it was reduced before the second performance.[10] The final chorus and the love-scene were abbreviated at the same period, whereas the scherzo, as indicated above, was lightly extended and the first (by then the only) Prologue was recomposed and the second definitively abandoned.[11] The latter, incidentally, was not disliked by any critic prepared to accept the first, and Heller liked it the better of the two (see Chapter 7 above, p. 65).

The critical battles of 1839

It is measure of the interest aroused by *Roméo et Juliette* that the 1839 performances were the subject of nearly fifty separate items – announcements, squibs, and reviews, often of considerable length – in the Paris press.[12] While many of them contain fair and detailed factual accounts, the reviews, as was normal when Berlioz came up for debate, reveal a striking disparity of opinion. Some critics praised Berlioz to the skies, others consigned his symphony and its genre to perdition; some accepted the programmatic elements as natural, even if novel, others questioned the right of music to usurp the role of chief bearer of dramatic ideas. The valuation of Deschamps' libretto was equally erratic, and whereas the variations in public response to the separate movements should surely have been a question of simple reporting, the critics' ideological imperatives led to differences even here.

In view of the twentieth-century tendency to deplore operatic elements in *Roméo et Juliette*, it may seem surprising that the least symphonic section, the finale, was unarguably successful. But the public was accustomed to hearing grand dramatic statements in the form of aria and chorus; despite being performed in a concert-hall rather than a theatre, the finale lacked the novelty value, or risk, of the symphonic sections. Even the most grudging critics agreed on the success of No. 2; and it seems clear that the scherzo also pleased the public, although some critics shunned it as merely bizarre. Not surprisingly this movement took the brunt of comments, among the clichés of Berlioz criticism, concerning concentration on the *fantastique* rather than musical substance, lack of melody, and a tendency to mistake colour and instrumentation for musical invention, a charge made by one critic about the whole work ('All its beauties are in the orchestration') long before it was applied to the scherzo alone by Hanslick.[13]

The success of this movement is a tribute to the Conservatoire orchestra. Alizard (the bass soloist) in particular, and the ensemble in general, were warmly praised, although it appears that the *Convoi funèbre* went badly on the first night. Both success and failure are variously attributed to the Introduction, the Prologues (including *Strophes* and the *Scherzetto*), and the *Convoi*; the *Scène d'amour*, fervently admired by Berlioz's friends, is generally agreed to have missed its mark, although performance and reception improved at the later renditions. Berlioz's remark (see above, p. 35) that most *musicians* considered it his best piece suggests that he may have considered it, like the *Tombeau*, caviar to the general.

For most reviews, the problem of genre, or as it was usually called, Berlioz's 'system', derives from Berlioz's invitation to regard *Roméo et Juliette* as a symphony. Clearly there was no precedent for such a work, and most people's ideas of genre were rather more rigid than one might expect in the early years of Romanticism. Moreover there was no unanimity, then as now, concerning the semantic nature of music. It is clear, even from the comments reproduced below, that critics had a *parti-pris* attitude to their work. For some, this meant for or (more vehemently) against Berlioz himself: the more honest included writers in Berlioz's personal circle, none of whom is completely uncritical. For others, general issues were raised concerning the nature of music as abstract, expressive, picturesque, or representational. Some took exception to the programmatic element altogether, others because the programme was too specific in its application: Berlioz met these part of the way by suppressing the second Prologue and simplifying the plot-content of the first. Some, not unreasonably, seized upon Berlioz's recent operatic failure; one accused him of writing a symphony in the manner of *Benvenuto Cellini*. Berlioz was assumed to be perverting Aristotelian theory (by which the arts are the imitation of nature) in the manner of the 'symphonies *caractéristiques*' of the eighteenth century: 'you can keep your libretto; I don't want to read in advance some loving translation of your violin phrases . . . let me dream at my ease, inspired by the delicious sensations your music will arouse in me, if it is any good'.[14]

Another criticized the entire project, on a generic principle: 'It is a mixture of symphony and opera without exactly being one or the other . . . Why cannot M. Berlioz give us a *Romeo and Juliet* opera?'[15] This was surely malicious; no one aware of the failure of *Benvenuto* could seriously ask such a question. However, this author claimed the support of the public who applauded only what was 'logical and regular' in the symphonic genre, rejecting the 'chaos without any distinct ideas' of the *Tombeau* (whose failure with the critics is not in dispute) and the bizarreries of the *Scherzetto* (which, however, other critics especially liked). But this critic wishfully misread the cultural situation: '[Berlioz] has the temerity to try to create musical Romanticism today, when literary romanticism is irrevocably condemned and Romanticism in painting is beating a retreat'. On the contrary, the 1840s proved to be the decade in which Romanticism became the established philosophy of French art: 'By 1850 many of the Romantic attitudes, vitiated and trivialized, had become respectable: the superiority of inspiration, emotion, and subjective judgements over tradition, rules, and skill was now official.'[16] Berlioz's *Roméo et Juliette* played its part in that development, although he himself never quite joined the establishment. As one 1839 critic put it, 'today's classic is yesterday's romantic'.[17]

By no means unsympathetic to the new genre (he begins his review by calling the work 'majestueuse et simple'), Paul Merruau concludes a thoughtful discussion more equivocally:

> By reducing music to some sort of language whose aim is to express a precise action or feeling, doesn't Berlioz realize that he is seeking to make poetry out of music . . . which is thus degraded to an unworthy role, becoming only the material formulation of feelings which do not originate within it? Pushed to its logical extreme, Berlioz's system would make the language of music no more than a matter of grammar, which everyone would talk equally well.

Whereas, he argues, the power of music resides in its ability to move us to 'delectable emotions' because it does not possess this degree of specificity.[18] Berlioz himself said much the same (see Appendix 1); but this critique suggests a deep unease with the concept of music even generally programmatic (an unease shared by Schumann in his review of the *Symphonie fantastique*, and reflected to some extent in Heller's review: see Chapter 7).

But the new genre had its defenders. *Le Ménestrel* reported twice on the new symphony.[19] At first the writer qualified a report on its success by declaring 'we have our reservations'. Nevertheless, 'The choral symphony from now on will be to the opera what the epic is to the drama; it brings into play the commentaries and episodes which the demands of the stage proscribe in the theatre.' And Joseph d'Ortigue claimed to find 'a mystical union of two distinct genres' in *Roméo et Juliette* between the drama in its entirety and the symphony with its 'majesty, grandeur, ardour, passion, variety of detail; with its scenes of gloom, of laughter and simplicity, its depictions of the visible world, its presentiments of an invisible world': a marvellously Romantic tribute to instrumental art, in the tradition of E. T. A. Hoffmann.[20] Even the musical novelties had their defenders. The sung programme, which in its original version verged upon the austerity of plainchant or eighteenth-century *recitativo semplice*, was praised for its 'cadences of historic colour . . . a strange effect not without charm to nineteenth-century ears saturated with perfect cadences and Rossinian formulae'.[21] The Prologue chorus also gave rise to a sterile argument as to whether it could be compared with the chorus of Greek tragedy (it cannot: the Greek chorus was not a narrator but an involved spectator, a role fulfilled only by the prologue chorus when it joins in the finale). Charles Merruau in the *Revue et Gazette musicale* evokes a Parisian public buzzing with questions on long-debated fundamentals of musical expression: 'must one condemn him because even his most poetic ideas take a descriptive turn . . . can one only be a great musician by adhering to the Italian school? is it heresy not to remain exclusively faithful to four-square rhythms? . . . to make cadences and half-closes less obvious by varying their form or eliding them, by avoiding repetitions in the melody . . . by mixing archaism with the most ingenious harmonic novelty . . . ?'[22] Whatever the genre, it is, according to Jules Maurel in *La France musicale*, 'one more added to musical poetics; [Berlioz] has drawn imitative music out of the little circle in which it was dying, and raised it to great, poetic, and well-characterized ideas.'[23]

Indeed, and despite Berlioz's indignation, for every harsh criticism of *Roméo et Juliette* in 1839 one can find a review filled with discriminating praise which should not be treated sceptically because it emanated from Berlioz's friends and associates, such as Jules Janin (who wrote for the *Journal des débats* when Berlioz's music was in question), d'Ortigue, Auguste Morel, or Stephen Heller. While some pronounce confidently that they are in the presence of a masterpiece, a work to be mentioned in the same breath with Beethoven, nearly all make some kind of reservation, of form or genre; and as we have seen, several precise criticisms anticipated Berlioz's own revision in the years preceding its publication. Not that he took all their advice: he did not, presumably, find the Introduction unsatisfactory because 'The musician's thought here is evidently sacrificed to the needs of the drama . . . it is all perfectly logical [from a dramatic viewpoint] but logic and music do not always walk together'.[24] This was Maurel, who was among several to notice the slight impression made at the first performance by the *Scène d'amour,* and who regarded what followed the scherzo as of less value, at least until the almost universally praised finale. But the material these criticisms supply is of such complication that I shall concentrate on two areas which have continued to arouse controversy into the present century.

The 'Réunion des thèmes' and the *Tombeau*

Berlioz noted in the score of the *Grande fête chez Capulet* that he had united the themes of the dance and the preceding Larghetto, 'Romeo's song'; this effect is anticipated in the overture to *Benvenuto Cellini*.[25] In view of the reception of this passage by certain later critics, it appears surprising that it was almost unmentioned in early reviews, which concentrated on the effective contrast between the slow and fast tempi, the implicit presence of Tybalt in the semi-chromatic ostinato, and on the applause the movement aroused. The following, however, clearly approves of the 'Réunion des thèmes':

> The ball scene, during which the oboe intervenes so ingratiatingly, is magnificently crowned by the general orchestral tutti above which the thundering voice of the trombones once more sings out the rustic melody that, a moment before, had so charmed the listeners.[26]

An otherwise unfriendly critic allows this movement 'great power; its motif has energy and even rhythm; it is developed effectively by a very bold brass effect'.[27] Richard Pohl later described the passage programmatically: 'Now the two hearts break out in love-jubilation, counterpointed by the sumptuously majestic dance music. Such a happy love forgets the whole world is around it!'[28]

None of these comments questions the propriety of a loud rendition of a theme originally heard within an intimate *piano*, and it might, indeed, be considered a characteristic effect of nineteenth-century music, the 'apotheosis' technique, of which examples abound in Chopin, Liszt, and other nineteenth-century music.[29] Yet this passage aroused the formidable ire of Ernest Newman, in keeping with his view of Berlioz (first expressed in 1905) as a genius of disastrous unevenness. In 1935 he took the 'Réunion' to illustrate Berlioz's proneness to 'failure of taste'; after painting

> the longing and the romantic heartbreak of his hero in an exquisite long-drawn oboe melody . . . he needs must bellow this same melody at us in the cornets and trombones for no logical reason that can be discovered: one wonders that Berlioz, of all people, with his rare ear for colour in conjunction with psychology, should not have seen that the melody is no longer the same thing when transferred from its first medium to its second. The procedure hardly makes dramatic sense at all, while it comes perilously near making musical nonsense.[30]

Strangely for one who espoused programme music, Newman recognized no change in Romeo's situation which might account for the new colouring of the theme. Possibly his objection was more musical than programmatic in origin, like Tovey's detection of a rhythmic fallacy; the reunion 'reveals what has already been open to suspicion, that the festive theme, for all its leg-shakings and twitchings, never had any power of movement at all': its speed is all surface, the harmony being static. David Cairns turns Tovey's criticism into a virtue; the ball theme 'seems both to whirl forward and to remain in the same place', a metaphor of energetic movement in a confined space.[31] More frequent performance, and understanding of its programmatic intention and musical architecture, may arouse enthusiasm for the movement not far from that of its first audience

The tomb scene, on the other hand, was questioned from the first, and Berlioz's advice that it could be omitted (see Appendix 1b) is less remarkable than his persistence in retaining it in the definitive version of the symphony. He must have had an abiding conviction, increasingly shared by modern critics, of its effectiveness and value. Few praised it in 1839; Maurel said it 'must be ranked with M. Berlioz's mistakes . . . we need a stage, scenery, tombs, theatrical half-light, people speaking and acting.' Auguste Morel commented that it 'would be perfectly adapted to a mime show which would make the action intelligible to the spectator. But I do not think the expression of such details belongs in the realm of the symphony.'[32]

Curiously, in view of what now appears the strident modernity of the music, more 1839 critics failed to mention this scene than singled it out for obloquy. One perversely liked both the *Convoi* and *Roméo au tombeau*, but his appreciation of the latter is based on a strange mishearing:

The song of the violins and the pizzicato of the cellos, at the moment of Juliet's awakening, freeze one with terror. This piece is broad and learned in construction.[33]

Berlioz's close associate d'Ortigue was differently chilled:

These elements [drama and symphony] are like two stars which can only shine on condition that they reflect each other: when one is in eclipse, all falls into darkness. I greatly regret to say it, but, whether from tiredness or from a theoretical error, this is what happens to the author in, of all places, for heaven's sake, the tomb scene: after a fine outburst from the orchestra, after a broad song for horns and bassoons accompanied by pizzicato double-basses, after Juliet's awakening, where the realism is a little too raw, we reach the moment of poison and the dagger-blow: the turning-point! the goal of the entire play! Yet here the composer abandons musical direction, following only that of the drama: no more poetry, no more ideality. I felt lost during some species of violin recitative, the depiction of the dagger-blow, the effects of the poison, the convulsions, the contortions, the stifled cries: it all left me cold.[34]

D'Ortigue's unfortunate reaction can be replicated in many subsequent commentaries; even Heller cautiously distanced himself from this movement.

In subsequent commentaries, the negative aspects – musical incoherence, excessive literalism – have tended to dominate the discussion. This movement has been singled out as beyond the pale of the permissible in programme music, even in two histories of the genre published early this century, in the period of Richard Strauss's ripest achievements. Friedrich Niecks (1907) called the young lovers' agony 'objectionable' and attributed the epithets 'confusing and ridiculous' to Felix Weingartner, the conductor and joint editor of the Breitkopf edition of Berlioz. Otto Klauwell (1910) excepted the *Tombeau* from his general praise of *Roméo*, and even Berlioz's warm admirer Tom Wotton (1935) sounds cautious in his reference to 'realism'.[35] J. H. Elliot professed himself baffled, finding only 'vaguely hysterical references to previous material', making it clear that he was either unaware of the real programme or did not wish to be guided by it.[36] In these circumstances it is perhaps not surprising that an influential modern defence of Berlioz should try to play down the programmatic element. Barzun says 'The twenty or thirty pages of the entombment are extraordinarily vivid and may induce visions in some listeners, but one can safely defy anyone to say what they imitate', a view which flies in the face of Berlioz's movement-heading.[37] In 1955, Newman echoed d'Ortigue in saying that Berlioz 'has on the whole failed to accommodate his symphonic intentions to his dramatic, or vice versa'.[38] As recently as 1972 A. E. F. Dickinson called the *Tombeau* 'musically confused', although others, such as Fiske and Macdonald, had clarified the issue by describing it in terms of Garrick's dénouement.[39]

Roméo et Juliette today

Roméo et Juliette is a work about which critical opinion seems unlikely to ossify. A standard view of it is expressed in the *New Oxford History of Music*: it has beautiful parts but makes 'a very unsatisfactory whole', which is only a more temperate version of Niecks's 1906 verdict: 'a monstrous jungle of incongruities'.[40] At least today one can be reasonably sure that opinions are formed in the light of musical experience. Full-scale performances of *Roméo et Juliette* have been an occasional feature of the concert scene since 1960, although the practice of performing extracts continues (and is, of course, authentic). The stylistic blend within *Roméo et Juliette* might be considered to make it an ideal work for recording; the disparities between symphony and opera are smoothed out when the forces used are no longer visible and all emerge from the same speaker(s). However, as much is lost. The visual and stereophonic elements of live performance cannot be captured on disc, and the disparities of scale – built, as Kemp argues, into a crescendo[41] – are part of the impact of a whole for which, perhaps, being satisfactory is no more a useful criterion than it is in a Mahler symphony; it may be no accident that the 1960s revival in Berlioz's fortunes coincided, at least in Britain, with the discovery of Mahler.

There have indeed been fine recordings, some associated with live performances, such as those of Pierre Monteux and Colin Davis in London, and Charles Munch in Boston.[42] Davis's pioneering performances with the Chelsea Opera Group, followed by *Faust*, *Benvenuto*, and *Les Troyens*, contributed to the Berlioz cult in Britain. And Roger Norrington's 'Berlioz Experience' (4-6 March 1988) climaxed with a performance of *Roméo* using a hall of the right size (the Queen Elizabeth Hall on the South Bank of the Thames), period instruments, and a disposition of forces based on Berlioz's prescription (Appendix 1c). Berlioz's electric metronome for co-ordinating off-stage forces with the main orchestra was replaced by closed-circuit television, a wholly appropriate anachronism which Berlioz would have enjoyed. As the dedication of this book makes clear, live performance must always have a role to play in understanding the true nature of such a work; the visible change of forces, while it may bespeak generic mixture, also encourages excited involvement. The effect, indeed, may reside partly in a sensed awkwardness, a consequence of the furious integrity of Berlioz's conception.

9

Afterword: Roméo et Juliette *as covert opera*

'*Roméo* est une symphonie': it lacks an 'action suivie', so although it may be dramatic in essence, it cannot be dramatic in form. Thus Jacques Chailley challenges us to defy Berlioz's own classification.[1] Yet *Roméo et Juliette* can only be understood as a symphony if we are prepared to distend that term beyond what is helpful. In 1839 Auguste Morel struggled to align it with a model: 'with the ball scene, the garden scene, the Queen Mab scherzo, and the finale, one has a complete symphony, cut virtually according to the pattern of Beethoven's Choral'.[2] Chailley's conflation of Nos. 1 and 2 into an introduction–allegro, and Nos. 5, 6 and 7 into a single composite finale, is no less specious; the last three movements interrelate music and drama in three different ways. Much as one may dislike the idea of a favourite work resulting from its creator being constrained by external events, Jeffrey Langford's statement that the dramatic symphony was a 'temporary substitute for opera' has the ring of truth.[3] Enough has already been said to determine that the case for calling it 'a symphony' *tout court* is negligible; in this chapter I shall try to make the case that it is best understood as a dramatic form, albeit one without precedent and virtually, as it now appears, without posterity.

Symphonies, as the *Fantastique* demonstrates, deal best with a dramatic development which is largely internal, a fantasy, the love it portrays being unknown to its object and unrequited. In *Roméo et Juliette* Berlioz assumes the objectivity of a dramatist; he deals not only with the mutual love of the protagonists but, departing (as we have seen) from his immediate sources, with society at large. That is almost in itself a sufficient reason for considering *Roméo* as a metaphorical drama, and only thus, I believe, can it be fully appreciated as a whole.

Wholeness is not the same as 'organic unity'; nor should every listener feel obliged to find it perfect. Its complicated nature, and the extent to which it is found uncomfortably mixed even today, deprive such claims of credibility. But a particular viewpoint can allow a perspective on the work which makes it critically reasonable to consider it, nevertheless, 'son oeuvre le plus génial',

80

as Messiaen has it.[4] And this viewpoint is consistent with Berlioz's aesthetic, and with his compositional interests and procedures. His language is not symphonic in the sense we understand from the largely Austro–German tradition; his music contains too many quirks to be considered 'abstract' or even as the bearer of a purely metaphorical and verbally ineffable narrative. Like a dramatist, he is always objective, but his aims are less imitative or representational than decorative and *expressive*; or, to put it more exactly, the music either illustrates a situation, like a Delacroix engraving of a Shakespeare scene, or it is imitative of feeling rather than action.

Such aims are uncomplicated in operatic music, in which action is indicated through words and music can concentrate rhetorically on atmosphere and character. It should be no surprise that Berlioz's finale, denigrated as Meyerbeerian in an age largely ignorant of Meyerbeer, won almost unanimous approval in 1839 (see Chapter 8). The modern critical acclaim of No. 6, denounced in the early reviews, is also suggestive. For what Berlioz *did* in *Roméo et Juliette* was to transfer his expressive language of instrumental music, already developed in two earlier symphonies and several overtures, to a framework of dramatic representation. This does not mean, however, that understanding, even of No. 6, should not be primarily in terms of feeling rather than imitation of an action, a point which may seem controversial but which I shall try to justify.

In opera, as Stephen Heller remarks, music comes first, just as it does in a non-programmatic symphony (above, p. 61). Deschamps clearly realized how strange a work he was caught up in; he wrote to Berlioz, on 21 June 1839: 'This will be something really unique, a *libretto* for a symphony! – an orchestra representing an opera!' And on 22 September Berlioz remarked that the work was 'the equivalent of a two-act opera' and contained fourteen numbers.[5] His original plans were probably operatic (see Chapter 2), and as late as 1859 he may have contemplated an opera on the subject, although all he said was that the idea could never be realized as no singers could match up to the demands of the lovers' roles.[6]

What genres, then, are mixed in *Roméo et Juliette*? Opera, undoubtedly and overtly in the *Convoi funèbre* and the finale; symphony, as discussed above; and programme music, with the proviso that part of the programme is sung. This idea may have seemed a natural development from the programme supplied to audiences for the *Symphonie fantastique*, which Berlioz compared to 'the spoken text of an opera [i.e. an *opéra comique*], serving to introduce the movements, whose character and expression it motivates'.[7] In 1836, another version of the *Fantastique* programme hints at the later work more directly:

'If the few lines of this programme had been of the kind that could be recited or sung between each symphonic movement, like the choruses of Greek tragedy, their purpose would surely not have been mistaken.'[8] This conception was put into effect in the original two prologues; but the final version adds a further generic mixture by allowing the Prologue chorus latitude for lyrical singing. And Berlioz eliminated not only the detail subsequently given by Lawrence but also the programmatic 'motivation' of his fifth and sixth movements.

A number of ambiguities and lacunae in the extant programme have been discussed already. They arose, no doubt, because Berlioz did not in any case believe that music could translate actions and words and still remain itself. With reference to Gluck's statement that the overture of an opera should 'indicate the subject of the action' Berlioz said simply: 'musical expression cannot go that far'.[9] The programme and movement-headings (which although not performed count as programmatic indicators) give the subject of each section, but Berlioz never intended a consistent relationship of programme to music; he wished to feed, as well as partly to control, the imagination. Some passages belong to the evocative, some to the narrative extreme of the programmatic spectrum; few (if any) attempt to replicate particular speeches, and musical coherence never depends on a precise correlation between music and play. To understand what Berlioz intended in No. 6 we need to know the events of Garrick's dénouement, but this does not mean that to follow the music we need the Garrick text open before us, nor that every phase of the movement should be accompanied by mental pictures or empathy with the verbally articulated consciousness of the characters; it does not even mean that we should attempt the feat of bearing these details in our memory as we listen. Such literalness is not only unnecessary, it may even distract the listener, as it clearly did several well-intentioned critics in 1839.

Roméo au tombeau is by some way the most representational orchestral movement, but its time-scale is operatic, not naturalistic; the invocation exceeds the time required for the action: it is an aria. There is no consistent relationship between the music and the action, nor is the programme necessarily more detailed than what Berlioz left in the score (see p. 52). Neither enjoyment nor understanding require us to consider such details as the death of Paris.[10] And yet this movement can be enjoyed on a musical level; Ian Kemp, indeed, calls it 'the most extraordinary music he ever wrote'.[11] The vitality of its invention, even as, or because, it flouts so many norms of its time, commands attention as a musical utterance: cryptic, perhaps, but possessed of enough musical coherence, even integrity, on motivic and harmonic levels, to satisfy a musical listening once the essentials of the programme – a frenzy of activity (arriving at and wrenching open the tomb), awe upon entering it, and so on – are clear. Do we need a literal explanation for the exact number of isolated chords beyond Berlioz's perception of how many neighbouring-chords to the dominant felt right musically?[12]

Having decided that the form may be dramatic, the questions which should be asked ('symphonie dramatique, que me veux-tu?') remain musical. In what rhetorical mode does this work address us? It is programmatic, but it does not follow that it is a redundant parallel to the play. In the *Scène d'amour*, Shakespeare's division into speeches, some short, some long, now one lover declaiming (unheard or as part of a dialogue), now both exchanging lines, is not formally musical; so Berlioz's music unfolds in long periods, analogous to but not reduplicating the dramatic dialogue. Tovey was right when he said that 'we shall be doomed to disappointment if we look to Shakespeare to explain anything we have failed to understand in the music' because 'the way in which his [Shakespeare's] words call up the right moods is quite incompatible with the way in which the music does so'.[13] Study of Shakespeare (or Garrick or Letourneur) may enlighten us as to *why* the music was written in this way and not another; but it cannot make it speak to us as music. If the music of the *Scène d'amour* strikes us as dramatic, it is through a metaphor. Musical eloquence arises from such factors as the exchange of melody between instruments in high and low registers and between lyrical and declamatory styles; the movement of harmony away from and back to points of reference, nearly all tonic; and the analogy to the development of Shakespeare's scene which lies in richness or thinness of texture, differences of tempo, rates of harmonic and colouristic change, and the development of motives.[14] To interpret programme music as if the sounds functioned like words is to interpret musical expressiveness as a background – a methodology not to be recommended even in opera.

Berlioz, in short, takes the play as programme; but his composition is not a detailed or critical commentary on it. He invites us to contemplate the well-known drama, or rather particular aspects of it; then to experience the workings of that drama upon him – and us – as musical beings. Chailley's assertion of symphonic primacy in *Roméo* directs us to consider Berlioz's music in musical terms, but it cannot seriously be maintained that *Roméo* is *just* music; if it can be enjoyed without recourse to dramatic interpretation, this enjoyment lies on one level only. Berlioz uses music to play directly on the listening mind, and he attempts to guide our responses by the extra-musical point of reference which, in his opinion, gave rise to the music in the first place. So, for example, the opening sections of No. 2 go deeper than the mere events required to symbolize the emotional growth of an adolescent (whose feelings were doubtless based on Berlioz's remembered experience): the self-absorption of the wandering opening, the gradual focus of feelings into eroticism, the focus of eroticism onto Juliet. Nothing in the music makes it clear that Romeo is in love for the first time (that particular Garrickism is irrelevant to the symphony), only that his love for Juliet is mature and convincing; as Berlioz observed, this is a love between equals.[15]

Berlioz structured *Roméo et Juliette* on novel lines, adapting his approach to the individual scenes he chose to include, and relinquishing any attempt at generic consistency in favour of a flexible design which combines relish of the moment with a forward thrust beyond the tragic end to final harmony. This argument tends to suggest that the paradigm for hearing *Roméo et Juliette* is, in a very special sense, concert opera. 'Opéra de concert' was a term Berlioz actually used while composing *La Damnation de Faust*.[16] *La Damnation* is no opera; but it is consistent enough in structure to be capable (with difficulty) of staging, whereas the imaginary theatre of *Roméo* is incapable of translation to the stage. Morel suggested staging the tomb scene as a ballet-mime: the other symphonic movements could not function in this way without a much more elaborate scenario than Berlioz supplied, and the Prologue is positively anti-theatrical. The Shakespeare prologues (or Greek tragedy) may have suggested 'Strophes', where Berlioz not only steps outside the action, but outside his own programmatic narrative, by invoking the name of the sublime author.[17] The original ending of the First Prologue ('Such are the first images and scenes which, before you, exploring uncharted ways, the orchestra will try to translate into music. May your attention sustain our attempt!') was omitted when the second was abandoned, but 'Strophes' contains a residue of this apology: if Shakespeare alone knew the secrets of young love (Berlioz seems to be saying), we have to accept inadequacy on my part.

Roméo et Juliette, with the excuse of being a 'dramatic symphony', does more than get rid of the trappings of visible staging. For the most part it dispenses with words and hence voices; moreover, as Chailley observed, it is indifferent to what is usual in opera, a reasonably intelligible succession of events.[18] This treatment of a drama does not, however, align *Roméo* with the later symphonic poem, a term which came to be applied to pieces in one continuous movement, and of which the obvious ancestor is the overture (*Coriolan*, *Le Roi Lear*) rather than the symphony. Berlioz's conception is less radical than this, or even than his own precedent, the *Symphonie fantastique*, an essay in autobiography without objectification, independent of sung text. Instead he sublimates his autobiographical involvement (with Estelle or Harriet) by a specific dramatic reference; and by having much of his programme performed, he forces the imagination of the listener into narrower paths than does a non-integral programme like that of the *Fantastique*. The closest relative of *Roméo* is not Liszt's *Faust* symphony, where three instrumental movements are sur-mounted by a choral finale, nor the 'Ode-Symphonie' developed by Félicien David (*Le désert*, 1844; *Christophe Colomb*, 1847), but César Franck's *Psyché*, a programme symphony with choruses and an instrumental Scherzo and *scène d'amour*.[19]

Berlioz compared his symphony to an opera in length, and it is also comparable in its thematic and tonal working, which has dramatic rather than structural motivation. The tonal and thematic relation of the introduction and finale is a case in point: formally, it has little significance (see Chapter 1, p. 5), dramatically it marks a turning point. This outer frame may not be the heart of the matter, but it is vital to the whole conception precisely because of its rhetorical lack of ambiguity; in this the Introduction, though without text, and No. 7 are gesturally typical of grand opera.

In the rest of No. 1, the Prologue, verbal narrative distances us from theatricalism. Having seized our attention with something externally dramatic Berlioz used narrative to modulate to the point where we can appreciate the internally dramatic. His procedure is consistent with the way that he considered Weber's and Beethoven's orchestral music to produce sensations which are 'not at all what one experiences in the theatre: there one is in the presence of humanity and its emotions; here a new world is opened up to view, one is raised into a higher ideal region, one senses that the sublime life dreamed of by poets is becoming a reality . . .' (see Appendix 1d). But Shakespeare could not be excluded from the ideal region; and Berlioz felt that the only musical medium fully worthy of the greatest poet was instrumental music without words. Hence his aim was to turn from the recognizably dramatic to the ideally dramatic; from the mimetic to the *expressive* musical ideal.

During the prologue, accordingly, rather than turning to symphony in the traditional sense, Berlioz sends opera under ground. *Roméo et Juliette* is an experiment in a new form, 'covert opera'. If the result is also a choral symphony, the contradiction is only apparent, for Berlioz was interested in the symphony not as a 'classical' formula but as the bearer of 'romantic' ideas. The blending of genres, in this light, is not surprising, for a thoughtful analysis of any nineteenth-century opera shows that the genre is hardly pure by nature. The reception-history of *Roméo et Juliette* suggests that problems have been felt both with perceptions of mixture of genre and mixture of quality. The latter must be largely subjective, and beyond the scope of reasonable discussion, but it is often dependent on the former: for instance, the qualities of the finale, where the public and private dramas merge, are those of grand opera, which for some critics has been enough to damn it without considering how well it works in its own terms. We have perceived in the discussions of the 'Réunion des thèmes' and No. 6 how divergent are reactions to avowedly programmatic music, and how they can depend on preconceived notions of propriety: for those with fixed opinions on genre, *Roméo et Juliette* is forever beyond the pale.

We need not be influenced by dogma in the face of such magnificent music. Berlioz's expressed conviction that the genre would not be mistaken (see Appendix 1a) may have been meant ironically, but he did not help by his negative definition: *not* an opera, *not* a cantata. Experience suggests that both these genres play their part. From the retrospect of the late twentieth century, after Franck, Mahler, Holst and Shostakovich, *Roméo* is not really a choral symphony; still less is it an oratorio. Yet it can be experienced as a coherent and successful whole if one takes the view that it stems from the natural form of musical drama, which is opera. The *Symphonie dramatique* should be redefined as a work whose nature is the refinement of musical drama for concentrated listening; an 'opéra de concert'.

Appendix 1

(a) Berlioz's Preface

Berlioz's Preface (originally printed in the libretto available at the 1839 performances; reprinted in the first vocal score, 1858). Large paragraphing from *NBE*, other divisions between paragraphs in the 1839 edition marked ¶ Material in [ ] is editorial; material in { } is in the 1839 libretto but not the 1858 score.

The genre of this work will surely not be misunderstood. Although voices are frequently used, it is neither a concert opera nor a cantata, but a choral symphony [*Symphonie avec choeurs*].

The voices are present almost from the start, but this is to prepare the mind of the audience for the dramatic scenes, whose feelings and passions are to be expressed *by the orchestra*. I also had it in mind to draw the choral forces gradually into the musical argument; if they appeared too abruptly they might damage the unity of the work. ¶Thus the {first} prologue, where following the example of {classical tragedy and} Shakespeare's own drama, the chorus gives an outline of the action, is sung by only fourteen voices. Later on we hear (from off stage) the chorus of Capulets (men) alone; then in the funeral procession, Capulet men and women. At the beginning of the finale the *two full choruses* of Capulets and Montagues appear with Father Lawrence; and at the close, the three choirs are united.

Only this final scene, when the two families are reconciled, belongs in the realm of opera or oratorio. Since Shakespeare's own day, it has never been performed in the theatre; but it is too fine, too musical, and it crowns a work of this nature too well, for a composer to think of treating it in any other way.

In the celebrated scenes in the orchard and the cemetery, the two lovers' dialogue, the asides of Juliet and passionate declarations of Romeo are not *sung* – in fact, the duets of love and despair are confided to the orchestra. The many reasons for this are easy to grasp. ¶First (and this would be sufficient justification on its own), this is a symphony, not an opera. ¶Moreover, the greatest composers have produced thousands of *vocal* duets of this kind; it seemed prudent as much as singular to try some other way of doing it. Then there is the very sublimity of this love, whose depiction by a musician is fraught with peril; his invention should be allowed the scope which the exact sense of sung words restrains, but which is possible in such circumstances with instrumental music, richer, more varied, less restricted, and thanks to its very indefiniteness, incomparably more powerful.

(b) Berlioz's note on *Roméo au tombeau des Capulets*

This note was included in the 1847 and subsequent printed scores.

The public has no imagination; pieces which only address themselves to the imagination have no public. The instrumental scene which follows is one such piece, and I consider that it should be omitted from every performance except those in which this symphony is presented before an élite audience extremely familiar with the fifth act of Shakespeare's tragedy with Garrick's ending, and with the most exalted poetic feelings: which is to say that it should be cut ninety-nine times in a hundred. It also presents exceptional difficulties to the conductor who wants to perform it. It follows that after the Juliet's Funeral Procession one should make a short silence and begin the finale.

(c) Berlioz's observations on performance

From the second impression of the full score, 1847

To perform this symphony, the best set-up for the choruses and orchestra is as follows:

In a large opera-house, like those of Paris, Berlin, Dresden, Vienna, London and St Petersburg, the pit normally used by the orchestra should be covered; this platform should be a foot and a half lower than the front of the stage. The footlights will be closed off. On the stage, place a large shell, extending roughly to the back of the stage; at the back of this structure, four risers each two and a half feet high. In front of these the stage should be clear to a depth of about ten meters. Since this caters for a total of 270 performers, the chorus of Capulets should be placed *on the right, on the platform over the pit*, and lower than the theatre stage; the chorus of Montagues goes *on the left*. The sopranos, in front, should be *seated*; the tenors and basses, on the other hand, will sing *standing*, so that their voices will not be muffled by the women in front of them.

The Prologue chorus, which may be twenty strong rather than only fourteen, will *stand* on the front of the stage (along the footlights), and consequently behind the choruses of Capulets and Montagues, but above them. The three soloists – contralto, tenor, and Friar Lawrence – will be in the centre with the Prologue chorus, but in front of them.

Quite near the Prologue and soloists will be the *conductor*. The whole mass of chorus and singers faces the public with their backs to the conductor, and so they will not be able to see the beat; but a *chorus-master*, at the front of the orchestra floor with his back to the public, facing the first rows of sopranos, can follow the conductor's movements and relay them to the choruses with complete precision.

The orchestra will be seated in the normal way. The first violins are stage right [i.e. left from the audience's viewpoint], showing their profile to the public, the second violins stage left, in the same way, looking across at the firsts. Between them are a double-bass desk and one of cellos, and two harps; all the rest of the orchestra is disposed normally on the risers, but taking care to place the violas near the front. The eight extra harps for the second movement (the *Fête chez Capulet*) can go in front of the two groups of violins, since the Prologue chorus will leave the stage once the prologue is finished. After the *Fête*, the eight harps can be removed, and their place is clear for the return of the small chorus and soloists, which only happens after the Scherzo and before the *Convoi funèbre de Juliette*.

I have explained, in a note at the foot of the score, how the male double chorus behind the scene should be performed [*Scène d'amour*]; there is no need for the chorus-master in charge to see the conductor; it is up to the latter to follow the chorus tempo, which he can hear easily.(*)

In the instrumental movement *La reine Mab*, it is better not to use all the strings, if there are a lot of them; at the most twelve or fourteen violins on each side, ten violas, ten cellos, and eight double-basses should play. In addition, for this movement, it is sensible to position the percussionists handling with the small antique cymbals in B♭ and F very near the conductor, and not on the last rung of the amphitheatre where they would normally be; without this precaution, the speed of the piece would infallibly make them fall behind at this distance. Finally, the choruses of Capulets and Montagues should not be seen by the public until after the instrumental Scherzo, during the interval which separates this piece from the *Convoi funèbre*.

Hector Berlioz

(*) The note in the score of No. 3 reads: 'This double chorus should be performed at the back of the theatre, or in a room adjacent to the orchestra; it is not necessary for the chorus-master to see the conductor's beat, as the audible horn cue from bar 35 will suffice. The conductor will follow the tempo of the chorus which he will hear easily. It is essential to have one or two violins or violas to give the pitch to the singers and prevent them going flat, as they will not be able to hear the orchestra while singing, as it is playing as quietly as possible.'

(d) Berlioz on the 'genre *instrumental expressif*

From Le Correspondant, *22 October 1832. For the original French see Condé,* Cauchemars et Passions *(pp. 97–8).*

A special genre of music, entirely unknown to the classics, but which has become known in France during the last few years through the compositions of Weber and Beethoven, belongs more firmly within Romanticism. ¶We shall call this the *expressive* genre of instrumental music [genre *instrumental expressif*].

In former times instrumental music seems to have had no other aim than to please the ear or to engage the intellect, just as modern Italian cantilena evokes a kind of voluptuous sensation in which the heart and imagination have no part; but in Beethoven's and Weber's works, one cannot miss the poetic thought, for it is ubiquitous. [. . .]

It is music which gives way to itself, needing no words to make its expression specific; its language then becomes quite indefinite, thanks to which it acquires still more power over *beings endowed with imagination*. Like objects half-perceived in darkness, its images develop, its forms become more unsettled, cloudier; the composer, no longer forcibly restricted to the limited range of the human voice, makes his melodies more active and varied; he can turn the most original, even bizarre, phrases without fear of making them unplayable, a problem one is always up against when writing for voices. From this stem the amazing effects, the curious feelings, the ineffable sensations, produced by the symphonies, quartets, overtures and sonatas of Weber and Beethoven. These are not at all what one experiences in the theatre: there one is in the presence of humanity and its emotions; here a new world is opened up to view, one is raised into a higher ideal region, one senses that the sublime life dreamed of by poets is becoming a reality . . .

Appendix 2

Texts of the Prologues and Finale[1]

(a) Prologue (final version); First Prologue (original version)

The figures dividing sections refer to the subsections in chapter 4 above, p. 24; they are not Berlioz's. Material in italics is in the original first prologue only, and is omitted in all printed musical sources. Spelling is modernized.

PREMIER PROLOGUE – PETIT CHOEUR
Récitatif harmonique

First Prologue (Small chorus)

(1)

D'anciennes haines endormies
Ont surgi, comme de l'enfer;
Capulets, Montagus, deux maisons ennemies,
Dans Vérone ont croisé le fer.
Pourtant, de ces sanglants désordres
Le prince a réprimé le cours,
En menaçant de mort ceux qui,
 malgré ses ordres,
Aux justices du glaive auraient encore recours.

Ancient slumbering hates
Have risen up as if from hell.
Capulets, Montagues, two enemy clans,
Have crossed blades in Verona.
However, the Prince has suppressed
These bloody riots,
Threatening death for any who,
 despite his orders,
Again have recourse to the justice of the sword.

(2)

Dans ces instants de calme une fête est donnée
Par le vieux chef des Capulets.
Le jeune Roméo, plaignant sa destinée,
Vient tristement errer à l'entour du palais;
Car il aime d'amour Juliette . . . la fille
Des ennemis de sa famille! . . .
Le bruit des instruments, les chants mélodieux
Partent des salons où l'or brille,
Excitant et la danse et les éclats joyeux –

In these moments of calm a party is given
By the old head of the Capulet family.
Young Romeo, bemoaning his fate,
Comes wandering sadly around the palace;
For he loves with adoration Juliet . . . daughter
Of his family's enemy! . . .
The sound of instruments, the pleasant singing
Wafts out of the salons where gold gleams,
Animating the dancing and the festivity –

[Musical citation: main theme of
ball music in two forms]

Poussée par un désir que nul péril n'arrête,
Roméo, sous le masque, ose entrer dans la fête,
Parler à Juliette . . . et voilà que du bal
Ils savourent tous deux l'enivrement fatal.
Tybalt, l'ardent neveu de Capulet, s'apprête
A frapper Roméo que tant d'amour trahit,
Quand le vieillard, touché de la grâce et de l'âge
Du jeune Montagu, s'oppose à cet outrage
Et désarme Tybalt, qui, farouche, obéit,
Et sort, en frémissant de rage,
Le front plus sombre que la nuit.

Forced by a desire which danger cannot inhibit,
Romeo, masked, dares to gatecrash the party
And talk to Juliet . . . and so both savour
The fatal intoxication of the ball.
Tybalt, Capulet's impetuous nephew, prepares
To attack Romeo, betrayed by excess of love,
When the old man, moved by the youthful grace
Of young Montague, prevents this outrage
And disarms Tybalt who, furious, obeys
And leaves, trembling with rage,
His brow darker than the night.

[Musical citation: ball music, ostinato
from bar 294, but starting on E♭][2]

(3)

La fête est terminée, et quand
   tout bruit expire,
Sous les arcades on entend
Les danseurs fatigués s'éloigner en chantant;
*Hélas! et Roméo soupire,
Car il a dû quitter Juliette!* – Soudain,
Pour respirer encore cet air qu'elle respire,
Il franchit les murs du jardin.
Déjà sur son balcon la blanche Juliette
Paraît . . . et, se croyant seule jusques au jour,
Confie à la nuit son amour.
Roméo palpitant d'une joie inquiète
+Se découvre à Juliette, et de son coeur
Les feux éclatent à leur tour.+[3]

(3)

The ball is ended, and when
   all its noise has died away,
We can hear under the arcades
The exhausted dancers going home, singing.
*Alas! Romeo sighs,
Because he is forced to leave Juliet!* – Suddenly,
To breathe again the air she breathes,
He vaults the garden walls.
Already on her balcony, pale Juliet appears . . .
And believing herself alone until daybreak,
Confides her love to the night.
Romeo trembling with anxious joy
+Reveals himself to Juliet, and from her heart
The flames leap up in response.+

[* to *: set to music from No. 2, bars 24–31]
[+ to +: set to music from No. 3, bars 367–71]

(4)
AIR – Contralto Solo

1er Couplet

Premiers transports que nul n'oublie!
Premiers aveux, premiers serments
   De deux amants
Sous les étoiles d'Italie;
Dans cet air chaud et sans zéphyrs,
Que l'oranger au loin parfume,
   Où se consume
Le rossignol en longs soupirs!

(4)
Strophes

First love that none can forget!
First vows, first declarations
   Of two lovers,
Beneath the Italian stars;
In this warm and breathless air,
Perfumed by the distant orange-blossom,
   Where the nightingale
Exhausts herself in long sighs!

Quel art, dans sa langue choisie,	What art, in its chosen language,
Rendrait vos célestes appas?	Can do justice to your heavenly beauty?
Premier amour! n'êtes-vous pas	First love! are you not
Plus haut que toute poésie?	Higher than all poetry?

Ou ne seriez vous point, dans notre exil mortel,	Or, in our mortal exile, will you not be
Cette poésie elle-même,	That very poetry
Dont Shakespeare lui seul eut le secret suprême	Of which Shakespeare alone knew the secret,
Et qu'il remporta dans le ciel!	And which he took with him to heaven!

2me Couplet

Heureux enfants aux coeurs de flamme!	Happy children with hearts aflame!
Liés d'amour par le hasard	Bound in love by the mere chance
D'un seul regard;	Of a single look;
Vivant tous deux d'une seule âme!	Living together within a single soul!

Cachez-le bien sous l'ombre en fleurs,	Hide it well amid the flowery shades,
Ce feu divin qui vous embrase;	This divine fire which burns you;
Si pure extase	Such pure ecstasy
Que les paroles sont des pleurs!	That its words are tears!

Quel roi de vos chastes délires	What king thinks himself equal to the
Croirait égaler les transports!	Transports of your chaste happiness!
Heureux enfants! . . . et quels trésors	Happy children! and what treasures
Paieraient un seul de vos sourires!	Can buy a single one of your smiles!

Ah! savourez longtemps[4] cette coupe de miel,	Ah, savour well this goblet of honey
Plus suave que les calices	Sweeter than the chalices
Où les anges de Dieu, jaloux de vos délices,	Which the angels of God, jealous of your joys,
Puisent le bonheur dans le ciel!	Pour out happiness in heaven!

(5)
REPRISE DU CHOEUR-PROLOGUE:

(5)

(with tenor solo)

Bientôt de Roméo la pâle rêverie	Soon Romeo's pallor and dreaminess
Met tous ses amis en gaieté;	Sets all his friends laughing:
'Mon cher, dit l'élégant Mercutio, je parie	'My dear', says elegant Mercutio, 'then I see
Que la reine Mab t'aura visité.'	Queen Mab hath been with you.'

Scherzino vocal –
TENOR SOLO ET PETIT CHOEUR:

Mab, la messagère	Mab, the light and
Fluette et légère! . . .	Airy messenger!
Elle a pour char une coque de noix	Her chariot is an empty hazelnut
Que l'écureuil a façonnée;	Made by the joiner squirrel;
Les doigts de l'araignée	The spiders' fingers
Ont filé ses harnois.	Have platted her harness.

Durant les nuits, la fée, en ce mince équipage,
Galoppe follement dans le cerveau d'un page
  Qui rêve espiègle tous
  Ou molle sérénade
  Au clair de lune sous la tour.
En poursuivant sa promenade
La petite reine s'abat
Sur le col bronzé d'un soldat . . .
  Il rêve canonnades
  Et vives estocades . . .
Le tambour! . . . la trompette! . . . il
  s'éveille, et d'abord
Jure, et prie en jurant toujours, puis se rendort
  Et ronfle avec ses camarades.–
C'est Mab qui faisait tout ce bacchanal!
C'est elle encore qui, dans un rêve, habille
  La jeune fille
  Et la ramène au bal.
Mais le coq chante, le jour brille,
Mab fuit comme un éclair
  Dans l'air.

And in this slender vehicle the fairy gallops
Night by night – in the page's brain
  Who dreams of mischief
  Or sweet serenading
  By moonlight under the tower.
Continuing her outing sometime
The tiny queen makes a landing
On the sunbaked neck of a soldier . . .
  Then dreams he of cannonades,
  Of lively ambuscadoes . . .
The drum! . . . the trumpet! . . . he
  starts and wakes
Then swears a prayer or two and sleeps again
  And snores with his comrades.–
This is Mab who makes this bacchanal!
And it is she again who makes
  The young girl dress up in her dream
  And takes her back to the ball.
But the cock crows, the day breaks,
Mab flies off like a lightning-flash
  Into the air.

(6)

REPRISE DU CHOEUR-PROLOGUE:
(au public)

(6)

Chorus (to the public)
[original first prologue only]

Tels sont d'abord, tels sont les tableaux
  et les scènes
Que devant vous, cherchant
  des routes incertaines,
L'orchestre va tenter de traduire en accords.
Puisse votre intérêt soutenir nos efforts!

Such are the first images
  and scenes
Which, before you, exploring
  uncharted ways,
The orchestra will try to translate into music.
May your attention sustain our attempt![5]

[final version only, with second prologue omitted]

Bientôt la morte est souveraine.
Capulets, Montagus, domptés par les douleurs,
Se rapprochent enfin pour abjurer la haine
Qui fit verser tant de sang et de pleurs.

Soon death rules our scene.
Capulets, Montagues, subdued by sorrow,
Agree at last to renounce the hatred
Which has shed so much blood and tears.

(b) Finale

CHANTÉ PAR TOUTES LES VOIX DES GRANDS CHOEURS ET DU PETIT CHOEUR ET LE PÈRE LAURENCE

Sung by all the voices of both large choruses and by the small [prologue] chorus and Friar Lawrence

LES DEUX CHOEURS
Quoi! Roméo de retour! Roméo!

Both families:
What! Romeo is back! Romeo!

CHOEUR DES MONTAGUS
Pour Juliette il s'enferme au tombeau
Des Capulets que sa famille abhorre!

Montagues:
For Juliet he shuts himself up in the tomb
Of the Capulets, his family's enemies!

CHOEUR DES CAPULETS
Des Montagus ont brisé le tombeau
De Juliette expirée à l'aurore!

Capulets:
The Montagues have broken into the tomb
Of Juliet who died this morning!

LES DEUX CHOEURS
Ah! Malédiction sur eux!
Roméo, Roméo, ciel! morts tous les deux!
Juliette, Juliette, ciel! morts tous les deux!
Et leur sang fume encore!
Ah! quel mystère affreux!

Both families:
Ah! Curses on them!
Romeo, Romeo, heavens! both dead!
Juliet, Juliet, heavens! both dead!
And their blood is still warm!
Ah, what a terrible mystery!

LE PERE LAURENCE
Je vais dévoiler le mystère:
Ce cadavre, c'était l'époux
De Juliette! – Voyez-vous
Ce corps étendu sur la terre?
C'était la femme hélas! de Roméo! – C'est moi
Qui les ai mariés!

Friar Lawrence:
I will unravel the mystery.
This corpse was once the husband of
Juliet! – Behold
This body extended on the ground:
It was, alas, the wife of Romeo!
It was I that married them.

LES DEUX CHOEURS:
Mariés!

Choruses:
Married!

LE PÈRE LAURENCE:
Oui, je dois
L'avouer. – J'y voyais le gage salutaire
D'une amitié future entre vos
    deux maisons . . .

Friar Lawrence:
I admit it;
I saw in this the saving token
Of future friendship between your
    two houses . . .

LES DEUX CHOEURS
Amis des Capulets/Montagus,
    Nous! . . . nous les maudissons!

Choruses:
Us, friends of the Capulets/Montagues!,
    Us! . . . we curse them!

LE PÈRE LAURENCE (Récit mesuré)
Mais vous avez repris la guerre
    de famille! . . .

Friar Lawrence:
But you went on with your
    family war!

Le jour où cet hymen en secret fut béni
Vit Tybalt expirant et Roméo banni.
(Au vieux Capulet)
C'était Roméo seul que pleurait votre fille;
Et dans l'aveuglement qui frappait vos esprits,
Vous la forcez, malheureux père,
D'épouser le comte Pâris!
C'est alors qu'elle vint me trouver: 'Je n'espère
'Qu'en vous, me cria-t-elle, il me faut un moyen
'De fuir cet autre hymen . . . ou bien
'Je me tue à vos pieds!' –

[final version only]
Pour fuire un autre hymen
La malheureuse fille
Au désespoir vint me trouver.
'Vous seul, s'écria-t-elle,
'Auriez pu me sauver,
'Je n'ai plus qu'à mourir!'

[both versions]
Dans ce péril extrême,
Je lui fis prendre, afin de conjurer le sort,
Un breuvage qui, le soir même,
Lui prêta la pâleur et le froid de la mort.

[CHOEURS: Un breuvage!]

J'écrivis aussitôt à son époux fidèle
De rompre son exil pour venir là, près d'elle,
A l'heure où renaîtrait sa vie
        avec l'amour,
Et l'arracher, tremblante, à sa tombe
        d'un jour.
Quelque hasard retint mon message
        en sa route,
Et je venais [tout seul] sans crainte ici
        la secourir . . .
[Mais Roméo, trompé par mille bruits sans doute,]
Mais Roméo trompé dans la funèbre enceinte
M'avait devancé pour mourir
Sur le corps de sa bien-aimée;
Et, presque à son réveil, Juliette informée
De cette mort qu'il porte en son sein dévasté,
Du fer de Roméo s'était contre elle armée

The very day this marriage was blessed in secret
Saw Tybalt dying and Romeo banished.
(To old Capulet)
It was Romeo alone whom your child mourned;
And in the blindness which overcame you,
You forced her, unhappy father,
To marry Count Paris!
Thus she came to find me: 'You are my only
Hope', she exclaimed, 'I must find some way
To avoid this second marriage . . . or
I shall kill myself at your feet!' –

[final version only]
To escape another marriage
The unhappy girl
In her despair came to find me.
'Only you', she cried,
'Can save me now,
Or I have no recourse but death!'

[both versions]
In this extreme danger,
I tried to change destiny by making her take
A potion, which, that very evening,
Lent her the pallor and chill of death.

[Choruses: A potion!]

I wrote at once to her faithful spouse
To defy his exile and come here, near to her,
At the hour when her life and
        love would reawaken,
And snatch her, trembling, from her
        day of burial.
Some mischance held up my letter
        on its way,
And I came here [quite alone] unafraid
        to help her . . .
[But Romeo, no doubt misled by rumours,]
But Romeo, misled in the field of death,
Had got here before me to die
On the body of his beloved;
And, as soon as she woke up, Juliet, finding
That he carried death in his broken body,
Used Romeo's dagger against herself

Et passait dans l'éternité
Quand j'ai paru! – Voilà toute la vérité.

And had passed from us into eternal life
When I arrived! – that is the whole truth.

LES VIEILLARDS CAPULETS ET MONTAGUS *(avec consternation)*
Mariés!

The old Capulets and Montagues *(with consternation)*:
Married!

LE PERE LAURENCE: AIR
(Larghetto sostenuto)

Friar Lawrence (Aria)
(Larghetto sostenuto)

Pauvres enfants que je pleure,
Tombés ensemble avant l'heure;
Sur votre sombre demeure
Viendra pleurer l'avenir!
Grande par vous dans l'histoire,
Vérone un jour sans y croire,
Aura sa peine et sa gloire
Dans votre seul souvenir!

Poor children for whom I weep,
Fallen together before your time,
Future generations will come to weep
At your dark dwelling!
Verona one day, without knowing it,
Will become a city of renown
And its suffering and glory will come
From your memory alone!

(Allegro non troppo)

(Allegro non troppo)

Où sont-ils maintenant, ces ennemis farouches?
Capulets! Montagus! venez, voyez, touchez . . .
La haine dans vos coeurs, l'injure
    dans vos bouches,
De ces pâles amants, barbares, approchez!
Dieu vous punit dans vos tendresses,
Ses châtiments, ses foudres vengeresses
Ont le secret de nos terreurs!
Entendez-vous sa voix qui tonne:
'Pour que là haut ma vengeance pardonne
'Oubliez vos propres fureurs.'

Where are they now, these bitter enemies?
Capulets! Montagues! come, look, touch . . .
With hate in your hearts, invective
    on your lips,
Villains, come near these pallid lovers!
God punishes you through your sensitivity,
His chastisement, his avenging flames
Hold the secret of our fears!
Can you hear his voice of thunder:
'If my vengeance is to pardon you on high,
Forget your anger.'

CHOEUR DE CAPULETS
(montrant les Montagus)
Mais notre sang rougit leur glaive!

Capulets:
(pointing at the Montagues)
But our blood reddens their swords!

CHOEUR DES MONTAGUS
(montrant les Capulets)
Le nôtre aussi contre eux s'élève!

Montagues:
(pointing at the Capulets)
And ours rises up against them!

LES CAPULETS
Ils ont tué Tybalt . . .
Et Pâris donc?
Perfides! point de paix!

Capulets:
They killed Tybalt . . .
And Paris?
Villains! no peace!

LES MONTAGUS
Qui tua Mercutio?
Et Benvolio?
Non, lâches, point de trêve!

Montagues:
Who killed Mercutio?
And Benvolio?
No, cowards, no mercy!

97

LE PERE LAURENCE *avec indignation*

Silence! Malheureux! Pouvez-vous sans remords,
Devant un tel amour étaler tant de haine!
Faut-il que votre rage en ces lieux se déchaine,
Rallumée aux flambeaux des morts!
 (avec une force croissante)
Grand Dieu, qui vois au fond
 de l'âme,
Tu sais si mes voeux étaient purs!
Grand Dieu, d'un rayon de ta flamme,
Touche ces coeurs sombres et durs!
Et que ton souffle tutélaire,
A ma voix sur eux se levant,
Chasse et dissipe leur colère,
Comme la paille au gré du vent!

FIN DE L'AIR

CHOEUR DES MONTAGUS
O Juliette, douce fleur,
Dans ces moments suprêmes
Les Montagus sont prêts eux-mêmes
A s'attendrir sur ton malheur.

CHOEUR DES CAPULETS
O Roméo, jeune astre éteint,
Dans ces moments suprêmes
Les Capulets sont prêts eux-mêmes
A s'attendrir sur ton destin.

LE PERE LAURENCE
leur présentant un crucifix
Jurez donc, par l'auguste symbole,
Sur le corps de la fille et sur le corps du fils,
Par ce bois douloureux qui console;
Jurez tous, jurez tous par le saint crucifix,
De sceller entre vous une chaîne éternelle
De tendre charité, d'amitié fraternelle;
Et Dieu, qui tient en main le futur
 jugement,
Au livre du pardon inscrira ce serment!

SERMENT DE RÉCONCILIATION
Nous jurons, par l'auguste symbole,
Sur le corps de la fille et sur le corps du fils,
Par ce bois douloureux qui console;

Friar Lawrence *indignantly*:

Silence! Sinners! How can you impenitently
Display such hatred in the face of such love!
Do you have to unleash your fury in this place,
Lit up by the candles of the dead!
 (with growing strength)
Good Lord, you who see the depths of
 our hearts,
You know if my wishes were worthy!
Good Lord, touch these hard and bitter hearts
With a ray of your glory!
At my prayer, may your instructing breath
Raise itself upon them,
Hunt down and scatter their anger,
Like grain before the wind!

Montagues:
O Juliet, sweet flower
In this awesome moment
The Montagues themselves are ready
To weep at your misfortune.

Capulets:
O Romeo, extinguished star,
In this awesome moment
The Capulets themselves are ready
To weep at your fate.

Friar Lawrence,
presenting the cross:
Swear, then, by the highest symbol,
On the bodies of your daughter and your son,
By this wood of sorrows, which consoles;
Swear all of you by the holy Cross,
To bind yourselves with an eternal chain
Of tender love, of brotherly friendship;
And God, who holds the scales of future
 judgement,
Will write this oath in the book of forgiveness!

Oath of reconciliation
We swear, by the highest symbol,
On the bodies of our daughter and our son,
By this wood of sorrows, which consoles;

Nous jurons, nous jurons par le saint crucifix,
De sceller entre nous une chaîne éternelle
De tendre charité, d'amitié fraternelle;
Et Dieu, qui tient en main le futur jugement,
Au livre du pardon inscrira ce serment!

LES MONTAGUS SEULS aux Capulets:
Et nous voulons par notre hommage,
Vous rendre Juliette encor:
Nous élèverons son image,
Toute brillante d'or!

LES CAPULETS SEULS aux Montagus:
Ah! que son Roméo fidèle,
Dans l'or aussi revive aux yeux;
Rayonnant toujours auprès d'elle,
Comme il rayonne aux cieux.

LES DEUX CHOEURS,
MONTAGUS ET CAPULETS
Nous jurons, par l'auguste symbole,
Sur le corps de la fille et sur le corps du fils,
Par ce bois douloureux qui console;
Jurons tous d'éteindre enfin tous nos ressentiments, amis! pour toujours!

LE TROISIEME CHOEUR-PROLOGUE,
AVEC LE PÈRE LAURENCE
Oui, jurez, par l'auguste symbole,
Sur le corps de la fille et sur le corps du fils,
Par ce bois douloureux qui console;
Jurez tous d'éteindre enfin tous vos ressentiments, amis! Ah!

LES VIEILLARDS SEULS
Allons! Frères!
Fêtons leurs noces funéraires!
Sur la tombe où vivront leurs amours,
Jurons-nous d'être amis pour toujours!

LES CAPULETS AUX MONTAGUS
avec un peu d'hésitation:
Amis! . . .

LE PERE LAURENCE
Le ciel attend!

We swear by the holy Cross,
To bind ourselves with an eternal chain
Of tender love, of brotherly friendship;
And God, who holds the scales of future judgement
Will write this oath in the book of forgiveness!

The Montagues, to the Capulets:
And to show our devotion
We will give you Juliet once more:
We shall raise her statue,
Gleaming in gold!

The Capulets to the Montagues:
Ah, may her faithful Romeo
Also live again before your eyes in gold;
Shining for ever beside her,
As he shines in heaven.

The two families,
Montagues and Capulets:
We swear, by the highest symbol,
On the bodies of our daughter and our son,
By this wood of sorrows, which consoles;
We all swear to end at last all our enmity, and be friends for ever!

The third choir of the Prologue,
with Friar Lawrence:
Swear, then, by the highest symbol,
On the bodies of your daughter and your son,
By this wood of sorrows, which consoles;
Swear to end at last all your enmity, friends! Ah!

The elders:
Let us go! Brothers!
Let us celebrate their funeral wedding!
On the tomb where their loves will dwell,
Let us swear to be friends in eternity!

Capulets to Montagues,
a little hesitantly:
Friends! . . .

Friar Lawrence:
Heaven expects it!

LES MONTAGUS AUX CAPULETS
avec un peu d'hésitation:
Amis! . . .

Montagues to Capulets,
a little hesitantly:
Friends! . . .

LE PERE LAURENCE
Dieu vous entend!

Friar Lawrence:
God hears you!

LES TROIS CHOEURS UNIS:
Amis pour toujours!

All three choirs together:
Friends in eternity!

(c) Text of the discarded Second Prologue[6]

DEUXIEME PROLOGUE –
PETIT CHOEUR
Récitatif harmonique

Second Prologue –
small chorus

Plus de bal maintenant, – plus de
    scènes d'amour!
La fête de la mort commence.
Chez le vieux Capulet, le deuil règne à son tour.
Juliette! . . . elle est morte! – Et la
    foule en démence
S'interroge. – Écoutez! – Ses soeurs,
    en ce moment,
Blanches, à travers les ténèbres,
En murmurant des cantiques funèbres,
S'en vont déposer saintement
La jeune trépassée en son froid monument.

No more dancing, now, – no more
    love scenes!
Death's celebrations begin.
At old Capulet's, mourning is now the rule.
Juliet! . . . she is dead! – And the
    crowd insanely
Is asking questions. – Listen! – Her
    sisters, even now,
Appearing white in the twilight,
Muttering funeral chants,
Are on their way to bury the dead young girl
In her cold mausoleum in holy ground.

[Citation from No. 5]

Roméo que personne encore
Dans l'exil n'a pu prévenir,
Croit morte celle qu'il adore;
Rien ne peut plus le retenir:
Il vole à Vérone, il pénètre
Dans le sombre tombeau qui dévora son coeur,
Et, sur le sein glacé dont vivait
    tout son être,
Il boit la mortelle liqueur! . . .
Juliette s'éveille!
Elle parle! . . . o merveille!
Oublieux de sa propre mort,
Roméo, comme dans un rêve,

The exiled Romeo, whom no one
Has yet been able to warn,
Believes his beloved dead;
Nothing can hold him back:
He hastens to Verona, penetrates
The dark tomb which will consume his heart
And, on the icy bosom where
    all his being dwells,
He drinks the fatal draught! . . .
Juliet awakens!
She speaks! . . . O miracle!
Forgetting his own death,
Romeo, as if in a dream,

Pousse un cri délirant, cri d'extase d'abord,
Qu'aussitôt l'agonie achève!! . . .
Et Juliette au coeur se frappe
    sans remord.

Un bruit vague et fatal remplit la ville entière,
La foule accourt au cimetière,
Appelant: Juliette! appelant: Roméo!
Les deux familles ennemies,
Dans les mêmes fureurs si longtemps affermies,
D'un saint moine, devant ce lugubre tableau,
Entendent la parole austère,
Et sur les corps, objects d'amour
    et de douleurs,
Abjurent, en ses mains, la haine héréditaire
Qui fit verser, hélas! tant de sang
    et de pleurs.

Utters an insane cry, at first of ecstasy,
Which his death-agony completes!! . . .
And Juliet without remorse stabs herself
    to the heart.

A sinister murmuring fills the whole city,
The crowd rushes to the graveyard,
Calling: Juliet! calling: Romeo!
The two enemy families,
So long locked into the same anger,
Before this gloomy scene,
Hear the austere words of a holy monk,
And over the bodies of those they
    love and mourn
Forswear, at his hands, their inherited loathing
Which, alas, spilled so much blood,
    so many tears.

Notes

1 Introduction

1 See Appendix 1a for the full text of the Preface, which was printed in the 1839 libretto. The term 'concert opera' was used by Berlioz in the early stages of composing *La Damnation de Faust*, but was finally rejected in favour of *Légende dramatique*.

2 Berlioz used the term 'genre *instrumental expressif*' in connection with a discussion of Beethoven's symphonies, in 'Sur la musique classique et la musique romantique', *Le Correspondant*, 22 October 1832 (D. Kern Holoman, *Catalogue*, article C18 on p. 436, partly reprinted in Condé, *Cauchemars et Passions*: see p. 97). In places the language of this article anticipates the Preface to *Roméo*; parts of it are reproduced in Appendix 1d.

3 Berlioz's concern with communicating his musical message led him to specify the precise physical disposition of his vocal and orchestral forces: see Appendix 1c.

4 The division of *Roméo et Juliette* into seven movements follows the 1839 libretto as well as common sense. Perplexity is sometimes caused by repetition of an error in the 1847 edition, whereby the headings of parts 5 to 7 are missing, suggesting that Nos. 4–7 constitute a unit. The old Berlioz Edition (*Hector Berlioz: Werke*, edited by C. Malherbe and F. Weingartner, Leipzig, Breitkopf and Härtel, 1900–7) compounded the error rather than eliminating it by inventing a subdivision into three large parts.

5 Auguste Morel, in *Le Constitutionnel, Journal du Commerce, Politique et Littérature*, 18 November 1839.

6 See J. Rushton, 'Le salut de Faust', in C. Wasselin and P.–R. Serna (eds.), *Berlioz Liber* (Paris: Plume, forthcoming); Ian Kemp, *Hector Berlioz: Les Troyens* (Cambridge University Press, 1988).

7 Shakespeare's second prologue, before Act II ('Now old desire doth in his death-bed lie'), concentrates on the problems the lovers will face in meeting, and thus prepares the orchard scene which follows; this is reflected in Berlioz's [first] Prologue, not in his rejected second.

8 An exception is Berlioz's *Symphonie funèbre et triomphale*, whose first movement is in F minor and last in B flat major, a procedure explained by the progression implicit in the title. In the nineteenth century there was no particular expectation that operas should begin and end in the same key, although some do, including Berlioz's *Benvenuto Cellini*.

2 The genesis of *Roméo et Juliette*

1 *Mémoires*, Chapter 18. On Harriet Smithson see Peter Raby, *Fair Ophelia*.

2 The *Hamlet* performance was on 11 September 1827, *Romeo and Juliet* on the 15th. Berlioz had been given a free pass through his friendship with Bloc, conductor at the Odéon: see David Cairns, *Berlioz*, p. 234.

3 Pierre Letourneur's translation was published in 1778 and revised by other hands up to 1821.

See Ian Kemp, '*Romeo and Juliet* and *Roméo et Juliette*', p. 42. Cairns says that Berlioz attended evening classes in English in 1828, and he became a fluent reader of the language (*Memoirs*, p. 97); he incessantly quoted Shakespeare in the original in his letters and published writings.

4   *The Illustrated London News*, 12 February 1848. Cairns (*Memoirs*, p. 97) says the writer was probably the paper's music critic Charles Gruneisen. D. Kern Holoman suggests that the story may even be true, but questions what conception of a symphony Berlioz might have had at this time (*Berlioz*, p. 46); Cairns says it 'cannot be true' (*Berlioz*, p. 45).

5   Cairns, *Berlioz*, p. 245

6   *Le Correspondant*, August–September 1829, articles C.14–16 in Holoman, *Catalogue*, p. 435. See also Cairns, *Berlioz*, pp. 287 and 294. The article on classic and romantic music appeared in the same paper the following year; see Chapter 1, note 2 above.

7   Cairns, *Berlioz*, p. 248.

8   Hugh Macdonald refers to this probable revision: *Berlioz Orchestral Music*, pp. 14–15.

9   Letter to Humbert Ferrand, 2 February 1829, *CG* 113 (I, p. 232).

10 'It was at this period that M. Hector Berlioz spoke to me of his projected dramatic symphony on *Romeo and Juliet* [. . .]. We worked out the plan for this work of music and poetry; melodies and verses flowed along, and the symphony appeared . . . ten years later.' This passage comes between references to the rehearsals and performance at the Comédie française (24 October 1829) of Alfred de Vigny's translation of *Othello*. E. Deschamps, Preface to *Macbeth et Roméo et Juliette*, pp. xiv–xv.

11 *Mémoires*, Chapter 35. The words 'éteindre la haine qui fit verser tant de sang et de larmes' are almost identical to the end of the Prologue of the eventual symphony: 'abjurer la haine Qui fit verser tant de sang et de pleurs'.

12 'I met him at the Villa Medici in 1832 . . . He was already considering making a musical work on Shakespeare's *Romeo and Juliet*, and he asked me to write the libretto . . . ' A. Barbier, *Souvenirs personnels et silhouettes contemporaines* (Paris: 1883), p. 230.

13 *Mémoires*, footnote to Chapter 36. The 'double attempt' is explained in a footnote to the footnote: 'This symphony does indeed contain a vocal *scherzetto* and an instrumental *scherzo* on Queen Mab'. Berlioz's astonishment, and Mendelssohn's if genuine rather than polite, is odd; it was by no means usual to write scherzos based on poetry. Mendelssohn's own fairy scherzo from *A Midsummer Night's Dream* was not composed until 1842.

14 It is generally said that Berlioz saw *Romeo and Juliet* only once, whereas he saw a number of performances of *Hamlet*. But Harriet invited Berlioz to see her in *Romeo and Juliet*, staged by her company, in January 1833; it is scarcely conceivable that he could have refused, and he looked forward to the event keenly (see his letter to Du Boys of 5 January 1833 (*CG* 307: II, p. 60; Holoman, *Berlioz*, p. 139; Raby, *Fair Ophelia*, pp. 137–9).

15 *Le Ballet des ombres* was published at the end of 1829 as Opus 2. Its history is otherwise obscure; no copy survives of the original publication.

16 Letter of 21 August 1829, *CG* 134 (I, p. 270).

17 See *Mémoires*, Chapter 25.

18 The ghost's speech is fictionally presented by the narrator/author as the inspiration of the Juliet/Cleopatra music, a remarkable example of Berlioz's tendency to group his favourite themes around music of which he was particularly proud.

19 *Mémoires*, Chapter 29.

20 He kept *Sardanapale* in order to perform it, and was thus able to destroy the MS when it suited him. On performances see Holoman, *Catalogue*, pp. 97–8, and Peter Bloom, 'Berlioz and the Prix de Rome of 1830'.

21 The oboe theme appears in the surviving MS fragments in the expanded metre of the *Fête chez Capulet* in No. 2 (see p. 31), but not combined with the dance theme, which is in $\frac{3}{4}$ time. See Bloom, 'Berlioz and the *Prix de Rome*', and Ian Kemp, '*Romeo and Juliet* and *Roméo et Juliette*' (the music is quoted on p. 56).

22 Kemp (*Romeo and Juliet*, p. 59) considers the evidence that the *Sardanapale* music was conceived for *Romeo and Juliet* to be weak, but Deschamps' story provides at least a thread upon which to hang this theory. The determination to proceed with *Roméo et Juliette* may have signed the cantata's death warrant after several performances, just as *Le retour à la vie* signed that of *Cléopâtre*.

23 Holoman, *Berlioz*, p. 260.

24 On publication details, see D. Kern Holoman, *Catalogue*, pp. 200–1, and *NBE*.

25 Berlioz and Camille probably had sexual relations before their formal engagement: see Cairns, *Berlioz*, p. 350.

26 In Italy Berlioz's major works were the compilation of *Le retour à la vie* and the composition of *Le roi Lear*. *Harold en Italie*, *Benvenuto Cellini*, *Roméo*, and *Béatrice et Bénédict* all have Italian settings; *Les Troyens*, arguably, is also nostalgic for Italy.

27 *Mémoires*, Chapter 49. Besides *Harold* the concert included *Le jeune Pâtre breton* and the *Symphonie fantastique*, and works by Gluck and Donizetti (see Holoman, *Berlioz*, p. 615).

28 The only source for this letter is the *Mémoires*, Chapter 49. While there is no doubt that Berlioz received the money, it was rumoured that the gift came indirectly from the owner of the *Journal des débats*, Armand Bertin; but although this version was believed by the eminent and disinterested Charles Hallé, there is no real evidence to support it (see Cairns, *Memoirs*, pp. 597–8 (note to p. 247)).

29 Paganini received the dedication of the symphony, but never heard it. He died in Nice on 27 May 1840.

30 Letter to Ferrand, *CG* 616 (II, p. 512). See also *Mémoires*, Chapter 49.

31 Berlioz says he 'wrote in prose all the text which was to be sung between the pieces of instrumental music; Emile Deschamps, with his usual charming obligingness and his extraordinary facility, put it into verse, and I began . . . ' The prose draft does not survive, but it seems that Deschamps passed over the last words (the finale) only in June. The date 24 January is on the autograph of No. 2. This account of the history of composition is based on Holoman, Foreword to *NBE*, *Mémoires*, and contemporary letters.

32 Letter to Dr Berlioz of 26 November 1839. *CG* 683 (II, p. 599). Charles Merruau, 'Concert de M. Berlioz', *Revue et Gazette musicale*, 28 November 1839.

33 He wrote to his sister Adèle on 20 December 1839 that nobody had previously dared to give three successive concert performances of a single symphonic work (Letter of 20 December, *CG* 697 (II, p. 616)). I am grateful to Katherine Ellis for pointing out the analogy with operatic practice.

34 Letter of 29 March 1841, *CG* 746 (II, pp. 684–5).

35 Probably Wagner came to the first or second performance (see Julien Tiersot, 'Berlioz and Wagner', *The Musical Quarterly* 3 (1917), pp. 753–92). Although he wrote a less than flattering review (see Chapter 8, p. 71), his autobiography leaves no doubt that he was profoundly affected.

3 Berlioz, Shakespeare, and Garrick

1 On Berlioz's reading of Virgil, see *Mémoires*, Chapter 2.

2 See Chapter 1, note 2 and compare Stendhal, *Racine et Shakespeare*, in *Paris Monthly Review of British and Continental Literature* (Nos. 9 and 12, 1823 and 1825), expanded and republished in 1827.

3 For detailed discussion of the Shakespeare season see John R. Elliott: 'The Shakespeare Berlioz Saw'; Peter Raby, *Fair Ophelia*, which includes a large selection of contemporary illustrations; Cairns, *Berlioz*, Chapter 14 (from p. 227), which discusses contemporary French Anglophilia; Kemp: '*Romeo and Juliet* and *Roméo et Juliette*'.

4 Berlioz refers to the Letourneur translation (see above, p. 7). There is also a translation of what

is referred to in this chapter as the 'Kemble' version, within the collection *Théâtre Anglais* (Paris, chez Mme Vergne, Librairie Editeur, 1827). This French translation 'conforming to the performances' was available in the theatre.

5 Stendhal, *Racine et Shakespeare*.

6 See Elliott, 'The Shakespeare Berlioz Saw'; Raby, *Fair Ophelia*.

7 Hugo's preface to *Cromwell* argues that Shakespeare should be a model for modern literature, whose paradigmatic form is the drama. Dumas' *Henri III* (in prose as Stendhal advocated) was successfully produced at the Comédie française in 1829, the year before Hugo's *Hernani*.

8 Act III scene 5.

9 E. Deschamps, *Macbeth et Roméo et Juliette, tragédies de Shakespeare*.

10 On operatic adaptations of *Romeo and Juliet* see Winton Dean, 'Shakespeare and Opera', in P. Hartnoll (ed.), *Shakespeare in Music* (London: Macmillan, 1964), pp. 145–54.

11 Berlioz, *A travers chants*, pp. 52–3. The other four he mentions are by Dalayrac, Zingarelli, Vaccai, and Bellini. This article formed part of Berlioz's review of a revival of the Bellini (*Journal des débats*, 13 September 1859); it is mainly a panegyric on Shakespeare.

12 *Les Francs-juges*, completed in 1826, was rejected by the Paris Opéra after a reading of the libretto, so that Berlioz's musical efforts, including the 1829 revisions, were wasted. See D. Kern Holoman, *The Creative Process in the Autograph Documents of Hector Berlioz*, pp. 215–36.

13 Berlioz first called his work *Ouverture de La Tempête*; when he incorporated it into *Lélio* it became *Fantaisie dramatique sur La Tempête*. The titles together anticipate Tchaikovsky's genre, 'Fantasy-overture', used for *Romeo and Juliet* and *Hamlet*.

14 Garrick's preface to *Romeo and Juliet* (1750).

15 For the most thorough comparison of versions, see Kemp, '*Romeo and Juliet*', pp. 42–4. There is no documentary evidence of Berlioz reading another translation than Letourneur's before 1843. Parts of Garrick's version survive into Deschamps' translation published in 1844.

16 This version (see note 4) was taken over by Charles Kemble from his elder brother, John Philip. There were other cuts, which do not affect discussion of the Berlioz symphony; see Elliott, 'The Shakespeare Berlioz Saw'.

17 Deschamps restored Rosaline in his translation but introduces new lines (I.iii) to show that Romeo is already in love with Juliet before the ball, but without knowing her name.

18 Garrick's dialogue for this scene is reproduced in *NBE*, p. 385.

19 Berlioz, *Mémoires*, Chapter 16; Deschamps, *Macbeth et Roméo*, p. 352, where he offers a prose rendering of Shakespeare's final scenes but improves Garrick (if hardly reaching the spirit of the original) with his own measured alexandrines.

20 Such Catholic emphasis would have been impossible for Shakespeare or Garrick in Protestant England. Emphasis on the religious context, like the framing tonality of B minor–B major, is possibly the source of Balakirev's plan for Tchaikovsky's *Romeo and Juliet*; Balakirev instructed his disciple to open with music suitable for the Friar. See David Brown, *Tchaikovksy: a Biographical and Critical Study*, Vol. I (London: Gollancz, 1978), pp. 181–4.

4 Exordium: *Introduction* and Prologue; *Roméo seul*

1 The answer is in the dominant, F♯ minor, but the first note is the tonic, B, not C♯; thus the spanning interval is a ninth, not an octave. This follows the conventions of tonal answer which elsewhere (as at the opening of *La Damnation*) Berlioz was happy to flout.

2 Ian Kemp suggests that the 'preposterous' trombone phrases stand for Old Capulet and Montague ('*Romeo and Juliet* and *Roméo et Juliette*', p. 59).

3 Beethoven had used instrumental recitative before, but the 'speaking basses' of the Ninth Symphony, their phrases later set to words, are the obvious model. In an article in the *Revue et Gazette musicale* in 1838 (Holoman, *Catalogue*, C 301) Berlioz speaks of the instruments

crossing a 'bridge' (the instrumental recitative of the Ninth) to join the voices. 'Speaking basses' I take from Tovey's description of Berlioz's overture *Le Roi Lear* (*Essays in Musical Analysis* IV, p. 84–6).

4 Something similar occurs in *Les Troyens*, Nos. 1–2, when Cassandra enters following the misplaced jubilation of the Trojans. See J. Rushton, 'The Overture to Les Troyens', *Music Analysis* 4 (1984), p. 131.

5 Compare the Prologue to *Les Troyens à Carthage* (see *NBE* 2c).

6 The original form of the Prologue had another thematic and tonal pattern: the main theme in B♭ major, then, in F major, the chromatic ostinato, which a passage of text later omitted associates with Tybalt. See note 25 below and Appendix 2.

7 The original prologue did not have this extract, which comes 'out of order' in relation to No. 2 (where it is heard *before* the ball scene).

8 This lapse from the purity of 'harmonic recitative' is the result of revision of the Prologue; the original version had no excerpt from the love scene itself, instead preserving simple recitative up to the beginning of 'Strophes'.

9 This relationship of minor and major triads connected not through a common root or direct relationship but through possessing the same pitch as the third degree (mediant), is typical of Berlioz's harmonic thinking. See Rushton, *The Musical Language of Berlioz*, pp. 33–7.

10 To my knowledge no one before Berlioz scored for cor anglais quite like this, without an oboe, treating it as an equal with all the other high woodwind.

11 The voice cannot be Mercutio's, since it refers to him: ' "My dear fellow", says elegant Mercutio, "I see that Queen Mab has been down your way" '. Thus the tenor and chorus together are quoting Mercutio, not (like the baritone Friar Lawrence) impersonating him.

12 The main subordinate key of the Scherzetto is A♭, also used in No. 4 (bars 531–49) and in such F major pieces as No. 2 of *Roméo*, and the 'Easter Hymn' and 'Air de Faust' in *La Damnation*.

13 A minor as the diatonic mediant of F represents an easy step to the second movement. The original prologue prepared it still more clearly by ending in C major; the symmetrical structures of Nos. 1 and 7 (b–a; a–B) therefore result from revision rather than advance planning by Berlioz.

14 Autograph: 'Bruit lointain de bal et de concert', a reading reproduced in *NBE*.

15 On this see Rushton, *The Musical Language of Berlioz*, pp. 188–93.

16 'Mal d'isolement [Sickness of isolation]' is essentially the subject of the third movement (*Scène aux champs*). See also Friedheim, 'Berlioz' *Romeo* Symphony and the Romantic Temperament', p. 105.

17 Edward T. Cone, in his record review (*Musical Quarterly*, 1953, pp. 476–7), develops this point about the exhaustion of a tonality (F), and ideas of multiple perspective in the movement as a whole.

18 For this interpretation see Ian Kemp, '*Romeo and Juliet* and *Roméo et Juliette*', p. 62 (but Berlioz's revised syntax suggests the concert and ball are combined in the Allegro).

19 Newman, *Berlioz, Romantic and Classic* p. 184. Several earlier commentators have suggested a programmatic association between this melody and the lovers, starting with Berlioz's associate Auguste Morel who called it 'Chant de Roméo' (*Le Constitutionnel*, 28 November 1839), which fits well with its recurrence in the Allegro; Romeo's song, of course, must concern Juliet. Wolfgang Dömling considers its appearance in the Allegro the 'apparent representation of Romeo's inner loneliness, as he must hide his love for Juliet in company' (*Hector Berlioz: Die Symphonisch-dramatischen Werke*, p. 93). For Jeffrey Langford, it symbolizes 'Romeo's intense longing' ('The Dramatic Symphonies of Berlioz', p. 96). See also Chapter 8 below.

20 The cellos, basses, and bassoons reach written d' (sounding an octave lower in the basses), with the lowest pitch otherwise the viola and second horn c. The ninth, therefore, lies above the bass, but it is far more strongly articulated and the theoretical justification for the passage (as distinct from its evident splendour) lies in its unfolding over a dominant pedal. Berlioz

considered the Act III Prelude in *Lohengrin* would have been improved by the removal of the 'fourth inversion of the major ninth' (*A Travers chants*, p. 327).

21 Rushton, *The Musical Language of Berlioz*, pp. 74–6, discusses the articulation of this section by its instrumentation.

22 Schumann remarked that 'his [Berlioz's] loveliest ideas are almost always stated only once, as if in passing' (Cone, *Berlioz: Fantastic Symphony*, p. 236).

23 This point is discussed in the analyses of this movement and the overture by Bockholdt, *Berlioz-Studien*, pp. 32–50, and Rushton, *The Musical Language of Berlioz*, pp. 194–6. Tom Wotton observes that Berlioz balanced these 'reunions' differently; in *Roméo* the whole passage is *forte* rather than *fortissimo* and the dance rhythm is only *mezzo-forte* (Wotton, *Hector Berlioz*, p. 158). This combination of themes has been severely criticized: see below, Chapter 8, pp. 75–7.

24 On this see Cone (note 17 above).

25 The identification with Tybalt is clear from the original form of the First Prologue (see Appendix 2); it was noted by several early commentators close to Berlioz (see Chapter 8) including Auguste Morel, Joseph d'Ortigue, and Richard Pohl.

26 In a remarkably effective final gesture, which nevertheless some conductors see fit to alter by adding brass, Berlioz ends with woodwind only on the last motivic gesture and final chord.

5 The heart of the matter: *Scène d'amour, La reine Mab*

1 *'Orchestre seul'* is in the 1839 libretto, not the printed score.

2 *Mémoires*, Chapter 46; Berlioz's letter to d'Ortigue from Prague, 16 April 1846, *CG* 1034 (III p. 335).

3 J. H. Elliot, *Berlioz*, p. 170.

4 Berlioz feared the singers might go out of tune and suggested that a few stringed instruments should play alongside the singers to keep them up to pitch: see Appendix 2.

5 See below p. 41; Rushton, *The Musical Language of Berlioz*, p. 41.

6 'Vague des passions' is the phrase of Chateaubriand used by Berlioz in the programme of the *Symphonie fantastique*. On Berlioz's sometimes idiosyncratic use of the metronome see Hugh Macdonald, 'Berlioz and the Metronome', in Bloom, *Berlioz Studies*, pp. 17–36.

7 On these mediant relationships see Chapter 4, note 9 above.

8 Note how the flute leaps an octave to join the oboe, an effect, in a good performance – it is particularly vivid in Monteux's recording – as piquant as it is original.

9 See *NBE*, pp. 410–11. These surviving extracts of four and five bars respectively began otherwise lost passages 'of unknown length' from bars 317 and 358 (both, incidentally, use the G–G♯–A motive in the bass). The second passage reaches the E♭ harmony which bar 358 evades and moves through C to A minor; but it does not connect to bar 358 of the final version. In his essay *Franz Liszt's Symphonische Dichtungen* (*Franz Liszt's Symphonic Poems*, in *Gesammelte Schriften und Dichtungen* V (Leipzig, 1888), p.193; trans. W. Ashton Ellis, *Richard Wagner's Prose Works* (London, 1894), p. 249) Wagner chides Berlioz for spoiling his fine musical ideas by a development which adheres too closely to the Shakespeare play. If his view was based on memories of the lost 1839 version it cannot now be evaluated.

10 I would like to appropriate Herbert Eimert's phrase 'inorganic vegetable inexactness' ('Debussy's *Jeux*', *Die Reihe* V (*Reports: Analyses*), p. 3). Edward Bass discusses the motives of the love-scene in 'Thematic Unification of Scenes in Multi-Movement Works of Berlioz', pp. 46–8.

11 The violins' reiterated e''' anticipates the rhythm and pitch of the bell in Juliet's funeral procession, No. 5.

12 The Paris *Charivari* (30 November 1839), presumably because the critic failed to read the programme, referred to the lines about the lark and the nightingale which are actually in the later (post-marital) love-scene. Barzun, who attributes this error also to Wagner, roundly

reproves Tovey for associating bars 333–4 with the nurse (*Berlioz and the Romantic Century*, I, p. 332); but it is hard to find any other explanation.

13 Frits Noske alludes to the use of the 'death rhythm' in the finale of *Roméo et Juliette*, making it clear that Berlioz belonged to the tradition which recognized this 'topos'. *The Signifier and the Signified* (The Hague: Nijhoff, 1977, reprinted Oxford University Press, 1990, p. 183).

14 This late expansion of the dominant, a key classically used in the earlier parts of movements, is characteristic of Berlioz: compare *Scène aux champs*, and *Le spectre de la rose*, itself closely comparable to the *Scène d'amour*; see Rushton, '*Les Nuits d'été*: Cycle or Collection', in Bloom, *Berlioz Studies*, p. 117.

15 Berlioz's direction is 'en faisant rebondir l'archet' (making the bow rebound) for which 'Saltato' is a fair equivalent: 'shorter and lighter even than spiccato' (Normal Del Mar, *A Companion to the Orchestra*, London: Faber, 1987, p. 38).

16 See Rushton, *The Musical Language of Berlioz*, p. 136.

17 Berlioz presumably did not know such precedents for a slow trio as Schubert's C major quintet.

18 Paul Henry Lang ranks it among Berlioz's 'most accomplished creations' because it is 'a *bona fide* Scherzo', *Music in Western Civilization* (London: J. M. Dent, 1942), p. 861. But even commentators more sympathetic to the whole conception (Dömling, Macdonald) implicitly agree, by excluding the scherzo from discussion of dramatic aspects of the symphony.

19 The tonal scheme proceeds by phrase as follows: D minor ending on the dominant (368, intervention of the violas with Scherzo material); D minor to F major (384, followed by the cello and harp music); the first repeated; then D minor to F♯ minor (413, the cello–harp combination returning to D major). The F major–F♯ minor coupling is another instance of Berlioz's 'pun' (Chapter 4, note 9 above).

20 See Beth Shamgar, 'Program and Sonority: an Essay in Analysis of the "Queen Mab" Scherzo from Berlioz's *Romeo and Juliet*', and Ian Kemp, '*Romeo and Juliet*' pp. 68–9, for different interpretations of the form and programme.

21 Subject, cellos, 431; at eight–bar intervals, answer, second violins, then subject, first violins.

22 The cut was to have begun with music resembling the cadence before the trio; bar 474 would have corresponded with bar 333 (see *NBE*, pp. 411–12).

23 An early critic (Hippolyte Prévost, in *Le Commerce*, 1 December 1839) noted sarcastically the composer's apparent error of topic.

24 Ian Kemp has the soldier pray 'modally if perfunctorily' at bars 611–4, an intriguing progression which could also be interpreted as Mab meditating new mischief. At least the prayer is in the programme; but Kemp goes on to say that Mab 'inspects' the girl and taps her on the shoulder with a wand (like a fairy godmother rather than a mischievous sprite) when the ball music is already over (bars 716–25).

25 The Scherzo with two trios is familiar (though not necessarily to Berlioz) from the eighteenth century. In not considering this episode a trio (contrary to Shamgar, see note 20 above), I admit its melodic distinctiveness; but it is too short, lacks any cadentially articulated form, and is followed by no substantial reprise of the A section. Richard Pohl also found two trios, and considered, rather bizarrely, that Schumann's scherzos were influenced by Berlioz. But Pohl identifies the second trio as the horn-dominated passage from bar 476 (*Hektor Berlioz*, p. 165).

26 Berlioz describes the antique cymbals (tiny brass or copper instruments tuned to definite pitches) and how to play them in his *Grand Traité d'instrumentation et d'orchestration modernes*. They are used with a similar dreamlike seductiveness at the end of Debussy's *Prélude à l'après-midi d'un faune*.

27 Henri Barraud, *Hector Berlioz* (Paris: Fayard, 1979), p. 313; see also above, note 18.

28 A similar conclusion was reached by Philip Friedheim: the dramatic incidents omitted from between Nos. 3 and 5 are summed up in the scherzo, as all are 'the work of the spirit of the irrational, one might say the absurd' ('Berlioz's *Roméo* Symphony and the Romantic Temperament', p. 107).

6 Tragedy and reconciliation: *Covoi funèbre*; *Roméo au tombeau*; Finale

1 An earlier intermittent pedal, also with a religious context and representing bells, is the slow movement (*Marche des pèlerins*) of *Harold en Italie*. Berlioz introduced this favourite idea into his article on the theory of rhythm (*Journal des Débats*, 10 November 1837); see Rushton, *The Musical Language of Berlioz*, pp. 111–14, and (on the form of the *Offertoire*), 121–6.

2 On Berlioz and the Golden Section, see Rushton, *The Musical Language* pp. 183–8.

3 This was a favourite way of ending a movement, particularly one with bell-pedals; compare the slow movement of *Harold en Italie* and the *Offertoire*.

4 Originally the second prologue bridged this tonal gap, and an interval does the work of disassociation. Heller's review (see Chapter 7) divided the work into two at this point. However, the deftly handled transition between F major and E minor is touching in itself.

5 On the tonally 'incorrect' answer, see Rushton, *The Musical Language of Berlioz*, p. 121.

6 The inspired interruption of the chiming by rests (♪♩♪♩♩|-♩♩), came to Berlioz so late that the original (♩♩♩♩|♩♩♩♩) was printed in the first edition; this revision is not mentioned in *NBE*.

7 In the 1839 libretto this appears as *Roméo au tombeau des Capulets. Invocation–Réveil de Juliette. Elan de joie délirante, brisé par les premières atteintes du poison–Dernières angoisses et mort des deux amans.*

8 *Mémoires*, Chapter 24.

9 Comparable effects occur elsewhere in Berlioz, notably during *L'Enfance du Christ*; in Part I the conductor is asked to beat out seven bars of silence, and in Part III held notes transport the listener from the dramatic scene at Saïs to the meditative plane of the conclusion. Such spatial effects are reminiscent of the Requiem, where the effect of vast distance is created by sparsity and separation of sounds from the orchestra, in No. 1 at 'Te decet hymnus' and particularly in the *Hostias*.

10 See above, p. 11. The rhythm in *Cléopâtre* is reversed from the normal (♪♩ rather than ♩♪). Here the subdivision of $^{12}_{8}$ observes the normal rhythm, but with accents on the quavers. In both the rhythm is carried by pizzicato double basses.

11 The D major chord appears in a Neapolitan relationship to the tonic, but is approached as a $^{6}_{4}$, which gives it tremendous cadential weight.

12 See Rushton, *The Musical Language of Berlioz*, pp. 92–107.

13 This is perhaps Berlioz's most modernistic passage; for once the cliché 'ahead of its time' seems exactly right. The arpeggio of fourths, foreshadowed in the *Ronde du Sabbat*, anticipates Schoenberg (*Kammersinfonie* No. 1); the obstinate reiteration of pitches in the treble register suggests Nielsen (opening of his Fifth Symphony).

14 Hugh Macdonald points out the resemblance to Dido's suicide (*Berlioz Orchestral Music*, p. 53). The draining away of strength is handled differently, but to similar dramatic effect, in Berlioz's first major suicide scene, the end of *Cléopâtre*.

15 The derivation of the oboe melody may be deliberately ambiguous. For Macdonald (*Berlioz Orchestral Music*, p. 53) it recalls the oboe solo in No. 2 But this partly depends on the notation – tied semibreves in a fast tempo – while intervallically the passage is closer to the end of the 'Invocation', which also surrounds tonic and dominant with chromatically inflected neighbour-notes.

16 See Appendix 2 and *NBE*, pp. 395–9.

17 The 1839 vocal score in Columbia University Library includes the direction 'en imitant le bruit d'une foule qui approche'.

18 Tonally this ends the allusion to A minor and prepares the next principal tonality, C minor, by resolving down to its dominant, G. Locally, this move is complicated by the short progression directed towards D♭ (37–8) and the wailing figure against a sustained tritone A♭–D (39–42) which rises to C♭, so that the resolution onto a G major chord reinterprets the C♭ as B♮: harmonically a 'mystère' worthy of the situation.

19 The narrative device of falling semitones recurs in *Les Troyens*, in the speech for Hector's ghost.

20 Bar 299ff. is faintly, and surely not significantly, reminiscent of the stirrings of the Allegro in No. 2.

21 The obvious Meyerbeer comparison is the oath for the blessing of the daggers in Act IV of *Les Huguenots*, but a more conciliatory oath at the end of Act II is also in $\frac{9}{8}$. A closer model for Berlioz, however, is Rossini's fine oath in $\frac{12}{8}$ near the end of Act II of *Guillaume Tell*, which is similar in form and harmonic breadth.

22 And a full-scale anticipation of the same motive in *Tannhäuser*.

23 *A Travers chants*, p. 71; Kemp, *'Romeo and Juliet'* p. 48.

24 From bar 446; compare Requiem, No. 1 at 'luceat eis'; Te Deum, No. 2 (also in B major) at 'Sanctus'.

7 A view from 1839 by Stephen Heller

1 *Revue et gazette musicale*, December 1839, pp. 546–9 and 560–2 (the latter headed 'Suite et fin'). *Neue Zeitschrift für Musik* 12 (1840), pp. 31–2, 34–6, 39–40, 51–2, 56.

2 Berlioz himself wrote about both these passages (*A Travers chants*, pp. 53 and 69).

3 These references probably include two of Berlioz's operatic favourites: the priestly trombones in Act I of Gluck's *Alceste*, the clarinet solo in Act II of Spontini's *La Vestale* (Julia's aria 'Toi que j'implore').

4 Heller alludes to Act III of Meyerbeer's *Robert le diable*, a bassoon passage which Berlioz cites in the *Grand traité*, and to the 'Wolf's Glen' scene in *Der Freischütz*.

5 Heller appears not to notice the thematic identity between the recitative and the fugue theme.

6 This anti-Italian sentiment doubtless pleased Schumann.

7 Curiously, Heller does not identify this theme with the previous oboe melody.

8 In fact clarinets (bar 286) precede the flutes.

9 Heller is not alluding to the words but to the simplification of the theme.

10 Some parts of this description might correspond to the final fifteen bars, but Heller must be referring to a section which Berlioz subsequently cut, possibly in part because of his criticism.

11 According to Berlioz's *Grand Traité*, he saw such instruments in the museum of Pompeii at Naples and tried them out there.

12 The bipartite division is made by the second Prologue; there may have been an intermission after the scherzo. The first article in the *Revue et Gazette musicale* ends here.

13 This line was transferred to the 'first' (only) Prologue of the definitive version (see Appendix 2). Heller's admiration for the second Prologue did not save it, and unless the full score is rediscovered this is the only hint we have of its instrumentation. Long considered lost, the music survives only in an important early vocal score, now in the library of Columbia University, New York.

14 This presumably refers to the 'second theme' (see Chapter 6 above, p. 49).

15 Berlioz took Heller's advice and omitted the passage (for which see *NBE*, pp. 392–3).

16 The omission of several lines reflects Berlioz's agreement with this criticism.

17 This does not strictly conform with the score.

18 Heller cites the text 'Et nous voulons par notre hommage / Vous rendre Juliette encor!', a passage later omitted.

19 As, indeed, it finally does, more or less: the next passage, to which Heller objects, is also omitted.

8 Performance and reception: 1839 and beyond

1 For this purpose No. 3 begins at the Adagio, bar 124, to exclude the Capulets' chorus. Evidently Berlioz would not have agreed that 'the conductor who dares to perform this scene without the introductory chorus . . . deserves to have his ears cut off' (W. J. Turner, *Berlioz*, London:

Dent, 1934, p. 218). Berlioz preferred to keep the movements in their original order; Pierre Boulez saw fit to play them in the order 3, 4, 2, to end with the loudest. Details of Berlioz's performances are derived from Holoman's invaluable list of concert programmes (*Berlioz*, pp. 615–25), and his *NBE* foreword.

2 Conductors to add No. 6 include Dmitri Mitropoulos (see Cone's review, *The Musical Quarterly*, 1953) and Riccardo Muti.

3 Berlioz documented his travels of the 1840s in the Paris press, reprinting the material in his *Mémoires* (Chapters 51, 53, 55 and 56). Letters referring to *Roméo et Juliette* are listed with summaries in Holoman, *Catalogue*, pp. 203–10.

4 Holoman suggests that the third 1839 performance may already have been cut (*Berlioz*, p. 615). Heller's report confirms the inclusion of other music (see Chapter 7 above), but makes no mention of cuts. Since concerts at that time were often of a length unfashionable today, *Roméo* may have been given complete; Berlioz will have had confidence, by now, both in his performers and his public.

5 Performing movements 1–4 makes sense with the original first prologue, which stops short of the *Convoi funèbre*. Nevertheless Berlioz performed movements 1–4, with voices, for his Paris Société Philharmonique in 1851, and at Baden in 1858.

6 Paris: Catelin, published at the end of 1839. 'Strophes' was also published in London in 1846, as 'First love's pure vows'. Holoman, *Catalogue*, p. 201.

7 Kastner (1810–67), composer, critic and theorist, had written appreciatively of *Roméo* in the *Revue et Gazette musicale* on 12 September 1858. Berlioz gave him the score on the 17th: 'you will forgive me, my dear Kastner, for offering such a manuscript, covered in wounds from campaigns in Germany and Russia. It is like one of those flags which, as Hugo says, return from war more beautiful because they are torn.' See *CG* 2312–14 and 2316 (V, 591–6).

8 *Mémoires*, Chapter 49. There was no complete performance in Berlin, nor, as it happened, in London, although one was planned in 1855; Berlioz was forced to abandon the choral sections. Nevertheless a note in *Mémoires* rescinds an earlier observation that *Roméo* would never be viable in London, with its shifting orchestral personnel, because of the intensive rehearsal required.

9 Dresden *Abendzeitung*, 14 and 17 June 1840, in Robert Jacobs and Geoffrey Skelton, eds., *Wagner Writes from Paris* (London: George Allen and Unwin, 1973); see pp. 129 and 131. In his autobiography Wagner admitted to feeling like a schoolboy beside Berlioz.

10 'Une coupure avait été faite dans le courant de la scène du père Laurence. Cette heureuse suppression a contribué au succès de la dernière partie . . . ' (*Le Ménestrel*, 8 December 1839).

11 The revised first Prologue, with its newly conceived anticipations of later movements, is written on paper purchased in Prague (see *NBE* pp. 401–9; Appendix 2 below). The love-scene revisions can be dated by the use of, for Berlioz, a new style of C–clef; this change is also visible in the autograph of *La Damnation*. See *NBE*, p. 400; Holoman, *The Creative Process*, p. 81; and *NBE* 8b (*La Damnation de Faust*), p. 479.

12 I am indebted to Leslie Horn, who gave me a copy of her dissertation written at Smith College, Northampton, Massachusetts, under the tutelage of Peter Bloom. Horn noted 47 items in 28 publications, to which Heller's article must be added (the first review in the *Revue et Gazette musicale* was by Charles Merruau).

13 *Le Journal de Paris*, 27 November 1839. 'If it were possible to have fine orchestration by itself – and not always a question of *what* is orchestrated – then *Queen Mab* would be a pinnacle of orchestral composition.' Eduard Hanslick: *Aus dem Concertsaal* (*Geschichte des Concertwesens in Wien*, Part 2, Vienna, 1870, p. 80).

14 'P. V. [Pierre-Auguste Vieillard de Boismartin]' in *Le Moniteur Universel*, 17 December 1839.

15 A long article signed 'A'; *La Gazette de France*, 1 December 1839.

16 Charles Rosen and Henri Zerner, *Romanticism and Realism: The Mythology of Nineteenth-Century Art* (London: Faber and Faber, 1984), p. 10.

17 Anon, in *L'Artiste, Journal de la littérature et des beaux arts*, 1 December 1839.
18 *Le Courrier Français*, 26 November 1839.
19 1 and 8 December 1839; the articles are unsigned but presumably by the same hand, probably E. Viel.
20 *La Quotidienne, Moniteur de l'Avenir*, 26 and 27 December 1839. D'Ortigue and Auguste Morel (see note 33 below) claim an identity of essence between symphony and play which is hardly tenable.
21 *Le Ménestrel*, 8 December 1839.
22 Charles Merruau in the *Revue et Gazette musicale*, 28 November 1839.
23 Jules Maurel in *La France musicale*, 1 December 1839.
24 *La France musicale* 1 December 1839.
25 See above, Chapter 4, pp. 31–3.
26 *Le Ménestrel*, 8 December.
27 [L. or M.] Escudier, *Le Journal de Paris*, 27 November 1839; it is not absolutely certain that he is referring to the 'reunion of themes'.
28 Pohl, *Hektor Berlioz*, p. 147.
29 See for instance Jim Samson, *Chopin; the Four Ballades* (Cambridge University Press, 1992), p. 67: 'The deceptive innocence of Theme II [of the fourth Ballade] is transformed into a powerful apotheosis'.
30 Newman's essay 'Berlioz Romantic and Classic' appeared in *Musical Studies* (London: John Lane, 1905). The passage quoted is from a review of *Les Troyens* in Glasgow, see Newman, ed. Heyworth, *Berlioz, Romantic and Classic*, p. 204. Newman returned to this theme in 1955: 'in a lapse into the worst taste imaginable, Berlioz thunders out the Romeo melody in the brass, thereby completely destroying its true character' (*ibid.*, p. 184); his 1955 appreciation of the oboe melody was quoted above, p. 30. Newman's view may be opposed to that of Edward T. Cone (see note 2 above).
31 Tovey, *Beethoven* (London: Oxford University Press, 1944), p. 65; Cairns, in Simpson (ed.), *The Symphony*, p. 227.
32 Morel, *Le Constitutionnel, Journal du Commerce, Politique et Littérature*, 28 November 1839. Morel was one of Berlioz's closest musical confidants over the following years, and one of his main correspondents from abroad.
33 Anonymous review in *Courrier des Théâtres*, 25 November 1839: the description corresponds to nothing in No. 6.
34 See note 20 above.
35 Niecks, *Programme Music in the Last Four Centuries* (London, 1907); Klauwell, *Geschichte der Programm Musik* (Leipzig, 1910); Wotton, *Hector Berlioz*, p. 158. It would be interesting to note how often, in the absence of recordings, these generally sympathetic critics had the chance to *hear* this music, whose effect must be particularly difficult to imagine from the score.
36 Elliot, *Berlioz*, p. 172.
37 *Berlioz and the Romantic Century*, I, p. 334. Barzun accurately defines the movement as without classic form, falling into four sections; but if it imitates nothing, why does he call it 'the entombment'? However, I have some sympathy with Barzun's view (p. 335) that 'visualization' may not have been the response Berlioz most wished to promote; see Chapter 9.
38 Newman, *Berlioz, Romantic and Classic*, p. 183.
39 Dickinson, *The Music of Berlioz* (London: Faber and Faber, 1972), p. 152. See Fiske, 'Shakespeare in the Concert Hall', pp. 192–5; Macdonald, *Berlioz Orchestral Music*, pp. 52–3.
40 Niecks, *Programme Music* pp. 259. Gerald Abraham, 'New Trends in Orchestral Music', in *The New Oxford History of Music*, Vol. IX (Oxford University Press, 1990), p. 30.
41 Kemp refers to Berlioz's discussion of the 'law of crescendo' as experienced in Beethoven's Ninth, and applies this 'law' to *Roméo*. Kemp, *'Romeo and Juliet'*, from p. 48.

42 Munch (second recording, 1962), RCA–Victor LD–6098; Monteux (1976), Westminster WGD 2002; Davis, reissued on CD, Philips 416 962–2.

9 Afterword: *Roméo et Juliette* as covert opera

1 Chailley, '*Roméo et Juliette*', p. 115.
2 See Chapter 8, note 32.
3 Langford, 'The "Dramatic Symphonies" of Berlioz as an Outgrowth of the French Operatic Tradition', p. 91. He continues: 'We might ask if it is not as much a symphony as an opera' (p. 92). I do not accept the suggestion on p. 94 that the prologue recitative is operatic – indeed, it is anything but operatic; this difference, however, does not affect the argument.
4 Cited in the epigraph to this book, Messiaen's words are part of an interview with Claude Samuel on *Turangalîla*, recorded in 1961 (Vega VAL 127).
5 This suggests, incidentally, that Deschamps did not actually write anything for Berlioz in the 1827–9 period (see above, Chapter 2). Deschamps' letter is *CG* 655 (II, p. 562). It is hard to see what Berlioz meant by fourteen numbers (*CG* 665; II, p. 579).
6 On the opera project see Holoman, *Catalogue*, p. 426.
7 For the original text see *NBE* 16, p. 3; translation with discussion, Cone, *Berlioz: Fantastic Symphony*, p. 21.
8 *NBE* 16, p. 170; Cone, *Berlioz: Fantastic Symphony*, p. 28.
9 'L'expression musicale ne saurait aller jusque là.' Essay on *Alceste* in *A Travers Chants*, p. 176.
10 Several commentators including Macdonald (*Berlioz Orchestral Music*, p. 53) refer to Paris. Ian Kemp (p. 75) details four sword-strokes with which Romeo despatched him. These appear in no literary source; his source, where Berlioz mentions *three* sword-strokes (*Mémoires*, Chapter 35), refers to Romeo killing Tybalt in an imagined opera. Although Paris is listed among the dead in the finale, he is not mentioned in the second prologue, and there is no reason to suppose Berlioz considered him as a presence in the music of the symphony.
11 Kemp, '*Romeo and Juliet*', p. 37.
12 Kemp ('*Romeo and Juliet*', p. 75) says Romeo 'surveys the tomb [and] sees three bodies . . . Paris (bar 36), Tybalt (bar 40) – and Juliet (bar 44)'. But according to Shakespeare Romeo has only just carried Paris's body into the tomb. Had Berlioz intended to recall Tybalt, he could have done so in the second Prologue, or had recourse to the Tybalt motive from No. 2 (an association eventually deleted from the first prologue). Moreover, as Kemp notes, Garrick suppressed Romeo's invocation of the dead Tybalt; yet it is in No. 6 that Berlioz specifically invokes Garrick as his source.
13 Tovey, *Essays in Musical Analysis* IV, pp. 86 and 89.
14 Kemp's parallel-text approach to Nos. 1 and 3 ('*Romeo and Juliet*', pp. 44–5 and 65–7) is ingenious, but would only convince if based on the lost original form of No. 3.
15 'Romeo ascends to the love of Juliet: they are equal, she is his equal, they are sublime'; whereas, in *La Damnation*, Faust *condescends* to love Marguerite. Letter to Adolphe Samuel, 22 December 1855, *CG* 2070 (V, p. 222).
16 See *NBE* 8b, p. 457.
17 The second point of exteriorization, in the finale, where Lawrence steps outside the drama to prophesy that Verona will owe its fame to the star-crossed lovers, is an indirect allusion to Shakespeare, although reference to a golden monument raised by the families was omitted from the finale; the monument, therefore, is the Shakespeare play – unless it is the Berlioz symphony.
18 Despite the reputation of opera plots as incoherent, the events are usually in an intelligible succession, which says nothing of how they are motivated.
19 Despite this lack of real progeny, the importance of *Roméo* should not be underrated in a purely historical sense. Chailley calls it 'une oeuvre-clef de l'histoire musicale' ('*Roméo et Juliette*',

p. 118). John Warrack writes perceptively of its effect on Wagner (in P. Burbidge and R. Sutton (eds.), *The Wagner Companion* (London: Faber and Faber, 1979), p. 112): the melody opening No. 2 hints at the *Liebestod*; the tail-figure of the love-theme appears in the *Tristan* prelude. Mention has already been made of anticipations of *Tannhäuser* and *Lohengrin*; to these we may add that the hectic development of the love-music in No. 6 adumbrates the technique of Tristan's delirium. Messiaen included *Roméo* among influences on *Turangalîla*; and it may have had a generally liberating effect on the concept 'symphony', leading through and beyond Liszt to Mahler and the twentieth century.

Appendix 2

1 The layout of the text is based on the 1839 libretto, with emendations to conform to the final version of the score. Passages omitted in the final version are italicized. The original conforms to a temporary phase of spelling, writing, for instance, 'amans' for 'amants'; this has been modernized.

2 This, the first major omission from the final version of this Prologue, leaves a large part of No. 2 without its programme.

3 1839: 'Se découvre, – et ses feux éclatent à leur tour'.

4 1839: 'savourez-la bien'.

5 This first conclusion leaves to the second Prologue the task of introducing the movements after the Scherzo. Its direct address to the audience, an apologia derived from Shakespeare's Prologue, seems curiously wrong in tone and the perfunctory ending, in C major with curiously modal harmonies, prepares the F major of No. 2 no better than the final version, which ends in A minor.

6 The music (first published in *NBE*, pp. 414–8: it had survived only in a manuscript vocal score, now in the library of Columbia University) is still more austere than the original first Prologue. The words, however, clarify Berlioz's programmatic intentions for Nos 5 and 6.

Select bibliography

Barzun, Jacques. *Berlioz and the Romantic Century* (Boston: Little, Brown, 1950; 2nd edn, New York: Columbia University Press, 1969)

'*Romeo and Juliet* in Music', in Bea Friedland (ed.), *Critical Questions* (Chicago: University of Chicago Press, 1982), 148–55

Bass, Edward C. *Thematic Procedures in the Symphonies of Berlioz* (unpublished dissertation, University of North Carolina, 1964)

'Thematic Unification of Scenes in Multi-Movement Works of Berlioz', *The Music Review* 28 (1967), 45–51

Berlioz, Hector. *A Travers chants* (Paris, 1862; ed. Léon Guichard, Paris: Gründ, 1971)

Mémoires d'Hector Berlioz (Paris, 1870; ed. P. Citron, Paris: Gründ, 1969; for the English translation, see Cairns)

Correspondance générale d'Hector Berlioz, ed. P. Citron. Paris: Flammarion, 1972– (five volumes published to date)

'De l'imitation musicale', *Revue et Gazette musicale de Paris*, 1 and 8 January 1837, translated by Jacques Barzun as 'The Limits of Music', in *Pleasures of Music* (New York: Viking, 1951), reprinted with omitted passages restored in Cone, *Berlioz: Fantastic Symphony*, 36–46 and (without omitted passages, as 'L'imitation en musique') in Peter le Huray and James Day, *Music and Aesthetics in the Eighteenth and Early-Nineteenth Centuries*, Cambridge University Press, 1981, 482–8

Bloom, Peter A. *Berlioz Studies* (Cambridge University Press, 1992)

'Berlioz and the *Prix de Rome* of 1830', *Journal of the American Musicological Society* 34 (1981), 279–304

Bockholdt, Rudolf. *Berlioz-Studien* (Tutzing: Hans Schneider, 1979)

Cairns, David. *Berlioz: The Making of an Artist* (London: Deutsch, 1989)

'Hector Berlioz', in Robert Simpson (ed.), *The Symphony* (London: Penguin, 1966)

The Memoirs of Hector Berlioz (ed. and trans., London: Gollancz, and New York: Knopf, 1969; revised edn New York: Norton, 1975, and London: Gollancz, 1977)

Chailley, Jacques. '*Roméo et Juliette*', *Revue de Musicologie* 63 (1977), 115–22

Cockrell, William Dale. *Hector Berlioz and 'Le Système Shakespearien'* (unpublished dissertation, University of Illinois, 1978)

Condé, Gérard. *Cauchemars et Passions* (anthology of Berlioz's writings) (Paris: J.–C. Lattès, 1981)

Cone, Edward T. *Roméo et Juliette* (record review), *The Musical Quarterly* 39 (1953), 475–8

'Inside the Saint's Head', *Musical Newsletter* 1–2 (1971–2); reprinted in *Music, a View from Delft* (University of Chicago Press, 1989)

Berlioz: Fantastic Symphony (Norton Critical Scores: New York: Norton, and London: Chappell, 1971)

Crabbe, John. *Hector Berlioz, Rational Romantic* (London: Kahn and Averill, 1980)

Deschamps, Emile. *Macbeth et Roméo et Juliette, tragédies de Shakespeare, traduites en vers français . . .* (Paris, 1844, also reprinting the libretto of Berlioz's *Roméo et Juliette*)

Dömling, Wolfgang. 'Die Symphonie als Drama. Bemerkungen zu Berlioz' Beethoven-Verständnis', in T. Kohlhase and V. Scherliess (eds.), *Festschrift Georg von Dadelsen zum 60. Geburtstag* (Neuhasen: Hänssler, 1978)

Hector Berlioz: die Symphonisch–dramatischen Werke (Stuttgart: Philipp Reclam, 1979)

Hektor Berlioz und seine Zeit (Laaber: Laaber-Verlag, 1986)

Dukas, Paul. '*Roméo et Juliette* de Berlioz', *La Revue hebdomadaire* 3 (December 1894), 464–72, reprinted in *Les Ecrits de Paul Dukas sur la musique* (Paris: Société d'éditions françaises et internationales, 1948)

Elliot, J. H. *Berlioz* (The Master Musicians) (London: Dent, 1938)

Elliott, John R. jnr. 'The Shakespeare Berlioz Saw', *Music and Letters* 57 (1976), 292–308

Ernst, Alfred. *L'oeuvre dramatique de Berlioz* (Paris, 1884)

Fiske, Roger. 'Shakespeare in the Concert Hall', in P. Hartnoll (ed.), *Shakespeare in Music* (London: Macmillan, 1964), 177–241

Floros, Constantin. 'Literarische Ideen in der Musik des 19. Jahrhunderts. Berlioz' Konzeption des instrumentalen Dramas', *Hamburger Jahrbuch für Musikwissenschaft* 2 (1977), 51–7

Friedheim, Philip. 'Berlioz' *Roméo* Symphony and the Romantic Temperament', *Current Musicology* 36 (1983), 101–11

Garrick, David. *Romeo and Juliet by Shakespear; with alterations and an additional scene: as it is performed at the Theatre-Royal in Drury-Lane* ([London], 1750); also in *The Dramatic Works of David Garrick*, Vol. II (London, 1768, reprinted 1969).

Gautier, Théophile. *La Musique* (Paris, 1911)

Holoman, D. Kern. *The Creative Process in the Autograph Documents of Hector Berlioz, c.1818–1840.* (Ann Arbor: UMI Research Press, 1980)

Catalogue of the Works of Hector Berlioz (Kassel: Bärenreiter, 1987)

Berlioz (Cambridge, Mass., Harvard University Press, and London: Faber, 1989)

NBE: Foreword to Berlioz: *Roméo et Juliette* (New Berlioz Edition, Kassel: Bärenreiter, 1990)

Kemp, Ian. '*Romeo and Juliet* and *Roméo et Juliette*', in Bloom (ed.), *Berlioz Studies*, 37–79

Langford, Jeffrey A. 'The "Dramatic Symphonies" of Berlioz as an Outgrowth of the French Operatic Tradition', *The Musical Quarterly* 69 (1983), 85–103 and Graves, Jane Denker. *Hector Berlioz: A Guide to Research* (New York: Garland, 1989)

Macdonald, Hugh. *Berlioz Orchestral Music* (London: BBC Publications, 1969)
Berlioz (The Master Musicians) (London: Dent, 1982)

Murphy, Kerry. *Hector Berlioz and the Development of French Music Criticism* (Ann Arbor: UMI Research Press, 1988)

Newman, Ernest. *Berlioz, Romantic and Classic*, ed. Peter Heyworth (London: Gollancz, 1972)

Pohl, Richard. *Hektor Berlioz: Studien und Erinnerungen* (Leipzig, 1884; reprinted Wiesbaden: M. Sändig, 1974)

Raby, Peter. *Fair Ophelia: Harriet Smithson Berlioz* (Cambridge University Press, 1982)

Rushton, Julian. *The Musical Language of Berlioz* (Cambridge University Press, 1983)

Shamgar, Beth. 'Program and Sonority: an Essay in Analysis of the "Queen Mab" Scherzo from Berlioz's *Romeo and Juliet*', *College Music Symposium* (1988), 40–52

Tovey, Donald Francis. *Essays in Musical Analysis* IV (*Illustrative Music*) (London: Oxford University Press, 1936)

Warrack, John. 'Berlioz and the Theatre of the Mind', *The Listener* 72 (5 November 1964), reprinted in Felix Aprahamian (ed.), *Essays on Music* (London: Cassell, 1967), 49–52

Wotton, Tom S. *Hector Berlioz* (London: Oxford University Press, 1935)

Index

Balakirev, M., 105 n. 20
Barbier, Auguste, 10
Barraud, Henri, 45
Barzun, Jacques, 78, 107 n. 12
Beethoven, L. van, 1, 2, 8, 9, 12, 15, 18, 60-1, 75, 85
   Symphonies: No. 3 ('Eroica'), 8; No. 5, 61; No. 6 ('Pastoral'), 1; No. 8, 61; No. 9 ('Choral'), 1, 2, 8, 22, 58, 60–1, 80, 105 n. 3, 112 n. 41
Bellini, V., *I Capuleti e i Montecchi*, 9, 17
Berlioz, H., works by (see also *Roméo et Juliette*):
   Ballet des ombres, 10, 45
   Béatrice et Bénédict, 17
   Benvenuto Cellini, 8, 12, 14, 17, 32, 73, 75, 102 n. 8
   La captive, 25
   Cléopâtre, 11, 53, 104 n. 22, 109 n. 10
   La Damnation de Faust, 4, 12, 21, 71, 84, 102 n. 1, 105 n. 1, 106 n. 12, 111 n. 12, 113 n. 15
   L'Enfance du Christ, 109 n. 9
   Les Francs-juges, 8, 17
   Harold en Italie, 12, 21, 26, 61, 69, 109 n. 1, n. 3
   Huit scènes de Faust, 8, 9, 10
   Requiem (*Grande Messe des Morts*), 14, 59, 109 n. 10, 110 n. 24; *Offertoire*, 47–8, 109 n. 3
   Le Retour à la vie (*Lélio*), 11, 17, 70, 105 n. 13
   Le roi Lear, 17, 84, 106 n. 3
   Sardanapale, 11
   Le spectre de la rose, 108 n. 13
   Symphonie fantastique, 1, 6, 8, 10, 12, 17, 26, 60, 61, 70; *idée fixe*, 21, 23; programme, 74, 81, 84; *Scène aux champs*, 27, 41, 106 n. 16, 107 n. 14;

   Ronde du Sabbat, 1, 32, 109 n. 13
   Symphonie funèbre et triomphale, 70, 102 n. 8
   Te Deum, 59, 110 n. 24
   The Tempest, 12, 17
   Tristia, 70
   Les Troyens, 4, 8, 12, 79, 106 n. 4, n. 5; 109 n. 14, n. 19, 112 n. 30

Cairns, David, 8, 76
Chailley, Jacques, 80, 83, 84, 113 n. 19
Chopin, F., 76
Cone, Edward T., 106 n. 17, 112 n. 30

David, Félicien, 85
Davis, Sir Colin, 78–9
Delacroix, Eugene, 16, 81
Deschamps, Emile, 9, 10, 13, 16, 18–20, 25, 36, 72, 81
Dickinson, A. E. F., 78
Dömling, Wolfgang, 106 n. 19, 108 n. 18
Dumas, Alexandre, 16

Elliot, J. H., 36, 78

Fiske, Roger, 78
Franck, César, 85, 86
Friedheim, Philip, 108 n. 28

Garrick, David, 15, 18–20, 25, 47, 54, 78, 82–3
Gluck, C. W. von, 15, 82, 110 n. 3
Goethe, J. W., 8, 15

Hanslick, E., 72
Haydn, Joseph, 15, 61
Heller, Stephen, 71, 72, 74, 75, 77, 81, 109 n. 4
Holoman, D. Kern, 11, 12

Hugo, V., 16; *Hernani*, 17

Janin, Jules, 75

Kemble, Charles, 16, 18–20
Kemp, Ian, 78, 82, 105 n. 2, 108 n. 24,
 113 n. 10, n. 12, n. 14
Klauwell, Otto, 78

Lang, P. H., 108 n. 18
Langford, Jeffrey, 80, 106 n. 19
Letourneur, Pierre, 7, 18, 83
Liszt, F., 43, 71, 76, 85

Macdonald, Hugh, 78, 107 n. 6, 108
 n. 18, 109 n. 14, n. 15, 113 n. 10
Mahler, Gustav, 5, 78, 86, 114
Maurel, Jules, 75, 77
Mendelssohn, Felix, 10, 103 n. 13
Merruau, Charles, 75
Merruau, Paul, 74
Messiaen, Olivier, 81, 114
Meyerbeer, G., 58, 81; *Les Huguenots*, 4,
 110 n. 21, *Robert le diable*, 110 n. 4
Monteux, Pierre, 78, 107 n. 8
Morel, Auguste, 2, 77, 79, 82, 86, 106
 n. 19
Mozart, W. A., 15, 61

Newman, Ernest, 30, 76, 78
Niecks, Friedrich, 77, 78
Norrington, Roger, 79
Noske, Frits, 108 n. 13

Paganini, N. , 12–14, 18
Pohl, Richard, 76, 108 n. 25

Racine, Jean, 15, 16
Roméo et Juliette
 No. 1 (Introduction), 1, 2, 4, 5, 20, 21–
  3, 33, 58, 62, 67, 72, 75, 80, 85
 No. 1 (Prologue), 2, 5, 13, 14, 20, 23–
  6, 29, 30, 33, 36, 39, 41, 43, 56, 57,
  61–5, 68, 70–1, 73–4, 82, 84–5
 No. 1 ('Strophes'), 24–5, 30, 39, 43, 62,
  70, 72, 84
 No. 1 (Scherzetto), 26, 44, 63, 72–3
 No. 2 (*Roméo seul*), 2, 5, 9, 11, 13, 19,
  20, 24, 26–34, 36, 37, 63–4, 70, 72,
  84, 106 n. 12; 'Réunion des thèmes',
  31, 75–6, 86

No. 3 (*Scène d'amour*), 2, 5, 9, 13, 20,
 24, 26, 29, 33, 35–42, 54, 62, 64–5,
 71, 72, 75, 83, 85
No. 4 (Scherzo, *La reine Mab*), 2, 3, 5,
 9, 10, 20, 26, 42–6, 49, 61, 65, 71,
 72, 75, 80, 85
No. 5 (*Convoi funèbre de Juliette*), 2, 19,
 20, 26, 47–52, 65–6, 71, 72, 81
No. 6 (*Roméo au tombeau des Capulets*),
 2, 5, 13, 20, 23, 26, 30, 37, 38, 52–6,
 66, 70, 77, 81, 82, 86
No. 7 (Finale), 1, 2, 3, 4, 5, 9, 13, 20,
 26, 56–9, 61, 66–8, 70, 71, 72, 75,
 80, 81, 85, 86
Concert suite, 5, 70
Second Prologue, 2, 20, 23, 26, 71, 73,
 109 n. 4
Sonata form in, 22, 26, 48, 50
Tonality in, 5–6
Rossini, G., 31; *Guillaume Tell*, 17, 110 n.
 21; *Otello*, 17

Samson, Jim, 112 n. 29
Schumann, R., 60, 67, 74, 107 n. 22, 108
 n. 25, 110 n. 6
Shakespeare, W.
 Hamlet, 7, 9, 11, 12, 103 n. 14
 Romeo and Juliet, 3, 4; Berlioz sees, 7–
  10, 52; Harriet Smithson in, 16–17;
  versions of, 18–20
Smithson, Harriet (Mme Berlioz), 7–10,
 12, 16, 17, 52, 85
Spontini, G., *La Vestale*, 110 n. 3
Steibelt, Daniel, 17
Stendhal (Beyle, Henri), 15–16

Tchaikovsky, P. I., 105 n. 13, n. 20
Tovey, Sir Donald, 76, 83, 106 n. 3, 108
 n. 12
Turner, W. J., 112 n. 1

Vigny, Alfred de, 16. 103 n. 10

Wagner, R., 14, 60, 71, 107 n. 9, n. 12,
 111 n. 9; *Lohengrin*, 107 n. 10, 114;
 Tannhäuser, 110 n. 22, 114; *Tristan
 und Isolde*, 41, 114
Warrack, John, 114
Weber, C. M. von, 85; *Der Freischütz*, 62
Wotton, Tom, 78, 107 n. 23